TOPOGRAPHY OF WAR

ASIAN AMERICAN ESSAYS

EDITED BY **ANDREA LOUIE**
AND **JOHNNY LEW**

First published in 2006
by The Asian American Writers' Workshop
16 West 32nd Street, Suite 10A
New York, NY 10001

"Vietnam Veterans Memorial" by Maya Lin is reprinted from
Boundaries (Simon & Schuster, 2000) by permission of the author.

This book is set in Cooper Old Style
Book and cover design: Jeffrey Lin

Printed by Cadmus Communications — Science Press

Library of Congress Number 2005922319

ISBN 1-889876-15-1

CONTENTS

Way Home, 2004, Jeffrey Lin.

Topography of War began five years ago with the modest observation that wars seem to play significant roles in Asian American "stories" — both the stories we make and the histories that make us. To say the least, global and local conflicts throughout the world have dramatically influenced Asian American immigration, diaspora, naturalization and assimilation. World War II, for example, which is frequently regarded as a "watershed" in Asian American history, produced considerable effects — both positive and negative — for many Asian American communities. More than 110,000 Japanese Americans were removed and incarcerated throughout the western United States shortly after the bombing of Pearl Harbor. Also, many restrictions on Asian immigration and naturalization were lifted and relaxed as a result of the war, especially for those considered "allies" in the war effort. For example, the Chinese Exclusion Act was repealed in 1943. And in 1946 the Luce-Celler bill granted naturalization rights to Asian Indian and Filipino immigrants.

For many Asian Americans, wars lurk not too far from the surface of our families' lives and memories. Even casual unearthings of pasts seem to uncover a war or two. Is there, then, a relationship between wars and Asian American "stories" that may be explored and articulated? Is there, for example, a *connection* between them of which we may speak? Given the variety of responses to wars the essays in this anthology constitute, we believe that if there is a relationship between wars and

Asian American "stories," it is best to speak of them not as "connections," but rather as "intersections"—like lines of longitude and latitude. Wars and Asian American "stories," in other words, do not come together to form a single point from which all the essays in this collection may be conceptually ordered. Instead, wars and stories intersect to form landscapes, with as many valleys as peaks, as many planes as points. It is, of course, in this sense that this anthology is a "topography" of war, which we hope provides a sense of the range and depth of the ways in which wars and Asian American "stories" — not to mention the essays themselves — come together.

—◊—

Clearly, wars "happen"—like a force that razes homes, lives, communities and families, burning them down in conflagrations of violence and politics, or for that matter building them up in the very same flames. But wars also "haunt," as if they had become absorbed and embodied in our histories and memories, lingering like odd creaks in our floorboards. And they haunt not because they are always *there* — insistent with their presence — but because they are also *not there*. Like ghosts, wars haunt with an ambivalence of presence and absence. The fifteen essays in this anthology address this very ambivalence of wars' relation to our stories. In this respect, these essays are not only documentary accounts of wars' events. They are reflective wanderings into kitchens, attics and closets. They are intimate archaeologies of homes possessed.

In Part I, the essays focus on the continued "presence" of wars. Divided into two sections —"Wounds" and "Legends"— the essays in Part I address how wars stay with us, in some cases long after battles have ceased. In "Wounds," for instance, Dora Wang's "My Tangerine Childhood" describes the author's dreams of *tao nan* — meaning "to flee, to flight for life." Despite the fact that Wang had never personally experienced a war, her dreams are haunted by images of violence and apocalypse, as if they were inherited from her parents. "[My father] had done everything that he could to shield me, to give me some other kind of life than the one he had known," she writes. "He had raised me in southern California, bought me blue jeans and a new car when I was a teenager, sent me to the best American schools. But I grew up knowing *tao nan*, anyway." In "Skin," Rahna Reiko Rizzuto explores the varieties of identities she has inherited from war, an inheritance in the form of "skin"—racialized and politicized—which her own children also inherit from her. And in Dang Ngo's photographs of the Karen people of eastern Burma (also Myanmar), Ngo exposes us to the effects of continuing conflicts on the Karen hill tribes.

The above three essays show the extent to which wars assert their presence in the form of "wounds": injuries upon the mind, the body, the land. However, in the next section, essays reveal the ways in which wars live on through the stories we tell, especially the stories of our heroes and martyrs. In these next essays, wars live on not in the form of wounds, but "legends." In Shymala Dason's "Without Anger," the "word pictures" her family creates of Japan's occupation of Malaya during World War II—part real and part "fairy tale"—intrigue Dason for their sanguine nature. In "Death of a Red Guard," Xujun Eberlein dramatically reveals how conflicts produce and celebrate their heroes and martyrs, and with changing currents, neglect them as they slip into obscurity. Similarly, Gary Reyes' photographs of Filipino American veterans document their battles—their "Last Battle"—with their own legacies.

In contrast to the "presence" of wars in Part I, the essays in Part II focus on the subject of wars' "absence": the repressive and oppressive silences of forgettings. In its first section, "Memories," Luis Francia's "Light and Shadow," a meditation on the act of remembering, enacts not only a history of war but a war over history. His essay refuses to allow the history of Spain's and America's imperialist involvement in the Philippines to be shaped by the "victors." As he writes, "Who controls my memory controls me. Will it continue to be written by the victors, by Hollywood, with its seraglio of seductive images and infinitely mutable happy endings?" John Vu, in "Crossing the South China Sea," recounts his family's harrowing escape from Vietnam by boat, a recounting that is his own refusal to forget the remarkable experiences of Vietnamese refugees. And two architects, Anooradha Iyer Siddiqi and Maya Lin, explore the complex issues—personal, public and political—involved in creating physical monuments to memory: one to thousands of people killed and missing in a war, one solely to her father.

In Part II's second section, "Recoveries," Michael Sandoval, Jennifer Estaris, Elsa Arnett and Christopher Lee each write about recovering the past — as well as recovering *from* the past — by embarking on explorations of research: they interview family members and friends, scour through old documents and images, or travel to past sites. These writers experience a sense of distance and alienation from their own pasts, which their essays attempt to bridge. "Old tragedies have no place in the prosperity of immigrants, especially of their children," writes Sandoval. "We are raised as if a veil has been drawn between the past and the present. The comfortable house we inhabit — all signs seem to say — has been won precisely because the limitations of the past have been overcome. Yet we know as children that there once existed this man who is now dead — indeed, the voices whisper, who was murdered, whose body was found, they say, in a puddle." In "Child of Two Worlds," Andrew Lam also writes about the experience of distance and alienation. His essay explores the geographical and cultural dislocation he experiences within himself as a *Viet Kieu*, a Vietnamese national living abroad: "The greatest phenomenon in this century, I am now convinced, has little to do with the world wars but with the dispossessed they sent fleeing: The Cold War and its aftermath has given birth to a race of children born 'elsewhere,' or of transnationals whose memories are layered and whose biographies transgress the borders."

In Asian American history, the brute "reality" of wars is undeniable. Wars have impacted the blood, bone and flesh of people's lives. The defining and redefining of U.S.-Asian relations within the rhetorics of war — as "enemies" or "allies" — have shaped the public images and roles of Asian Americans. They have affected the public welfare of Asian American communities, initiating institutional changes in U.S. policies toward Asian immigration and naturalization. And years and generations later, miles or continents apart, wars continue to intersect with the ways we narrate and imagine our experiences and identities. We are entwined, in other words, in the *hauntings* of wars. For wars continue to inform our experiences of geography and "place" — if not with the immediacy of fire and shrapnel, laws and barbed wire, then with the ineffable yet undeniable hauntings of our histories and memories.

— New York, 2005

PART I. PRESENCE

WOUNDS

The author's mother as a girl in China, along with parents and brother.

The author's grandparents during wartime China.

MY TANGERINE CHILDHOOD

by Dora Wang

September 12, 2001. The streets outside are sparse, as if arising from a deep sleep, not yet certain if they are ready to wake. Late on a Wednesday morning, most of the stores in my friend Amy's Chelsea neighborhood are still closed, their glass doors shut tight behind steel screens. Even the newspaper racks are drowsy, still holding *The New York Times* from yesterday, September 11. Pedestrians walk in the middle of the streets, as cars are few and rules are suspended. Sirens echo through quiet air. We hear on TV that the gym is now a hospital, and Chelsea Piers, a morgue.

Even Amy's son, Will, four years old and walking between us, knows something is wrong. He is silent, and he is stirring with questions he is trying not to ask. He accompanies Amy and me as we finally venture outside her apartment to get groceries at the neighborhood Gristedes. He holds her hand as told and is careful to not wander from us. Will is already a young man, polite and helpful, aware of the world around him. His baby sister, Anna, who cries when afraid and laughs when happy, doesn't care yet if milk-scented drool spills from her cheeks onto mine. We left her playing in the living room back home, cooing among colorful blocks and stuffed rabbits, her blue eyes alert and alive, her plump hands clapping and reaching for her father. Throughout the sirens and eerie silences of the previous day, I kissed her and smiled, "Thank God for Anna!"

I am a visitor to New York, and I really shouldn't be here at all. New York friends who are away express dismay that they are not here, as if they are absent during a beloved friend's surgery or divorce, absent from witnessing a defining moment in the life of a cherished one. It was not Maritza or Monique who saw the World Trade Center explode and crumble to the ground yesterday after the attack by hijacked 747s, but me, when I emerged from the Broadway/Lafayette subway station just in time to see Tower Two transform into a column of smoke and ash. I wasn't sure of what I was seeing and I didn't ask, not eager to speak to strangers. A disheveled man sleeping in the doorway of the Barnes & Noble finally told me, and I thought he was only dreaming.

At Gristedes, the shelves are half empty, and the meat department hardly has anything at all.

"Three weeks' worth of rice, oil and salt," I say to Amy. "It's what my mother always told me. In times of war, you need three weeks' worth of rice, oil and salt."

Amy laughs, her light-brown eyes amused. With her small childlike hands, she picks up some yogurt along with enough orange juice and pasta to last the next few days. With Will skipping between us, we head back to her apartment.

Later that day, I phone my mother again to assure her that I am all right.

"*Aiya*, Bao Bao," she always calls me by this baby name. "Don't take public transport, no plane, train or buses. Rent a car and you drive. You and Chris take turn," she refers to my husband. "As soon as you can, just drive home to Albuquerque. There is nothing there. You will be safe. I was lucky. War has not really affected my life," she lies. "But I remember from when I was a little girl. I know how to do war."

"Yes, you taught me well, Mom," I say. "I know how to do war, too. I told my friend Amy to buy three weeks' worth of rice, oil and salt."

"Three months," she says. "Three weeks not enough."

"Oh my goodness, I got it wrong."

Standing in Amy's clean, modern kitchen, I hang up the phone. I picture my mother in her big house with the swimming pool out back, but wearing my brother's faded blue flannel shirt from his elementary school days, almost thirty years ago. Her kitchen broom closet is packed floor to ceiling with used plastic grocery bags, just in case there's an emergency and she'll need a few dozen of them. If the local supermarkets stop receiving food, Mom has enough vegetables and fruit growing in the backyard to last for weeks. She wanted all her kids to be doctors because if there's a war, doctors will always have jobs.

—⟋⟍⟋—

A war never ends. Its feeling lingers,
seeped into the land and into the people of the land.
War is in the blood and milk passed from mother to child.
I have never seen war, but I have always known the taste of it.

I wrote these lines in Los Angeles, the city where I grew up and where my parents still live, the place that I've come to call home, even though I now live in Albuquerque, New Mexico. Perhaps I wrote these words during an afternoon at Santa Monica Beach, taking in warm rays and ocean sounds before meeting friends for dinner on Montana Avenue. Maybe I was in Pasadena, enjoying classical music and a café au lait at Starbucks before browsing for shoes at Saks. Perhaps I was sitting next to the pool underneath Mom's grove of papaya in a neighborhood of streets lined with majestic old trees whose leaves are never shed in this land of no winter.

Los Angeles forgets, erases its past like no other city and prides itself on the manufacture of realities for the world to consume. Overnight in Hollywood, out of cardboard and paint, they construct Paris, London, Hong Kong or Beijing. In Los Angeles, place doesn't matter, just the sunny belief in endless possibility.

At home in a quiet suburb, Mom pushes a button on the remote control and watches Fred Astaire and Ginger Rogers dance across her living room. She loses herself in kisses between Clark Gable and Carole Lombard. She flips channels and finds herself on a busy street in Taipei, on a sunny island in the Mediterranean, in ancient Rome at the Coliseum, or in the melodic Rogers and Hammerstein South Pacific. There's no need to remember that she was a child in Nanjing in the days before the massacre, or that when she lived in Chongqing, bombs rained from the sky every afternoon. At the end of the day when the sun faded, her city burned tangerine, the color of fire at night, the color that would paint the days and nights of my own childhood.

On the block where my family lived in Montebello, another one of many temporary destinations that we called home, no one talked of war. Not Zohrab's family who had escaped the Armenian genocide, nor Tsutomu's family who survived the bombing of Hiroshima, not the Carlisles descended from slaves and sharecroppers, and not the Trasks who were among the very few Native Americans still left in the San Gabriel Valley. We were Americans, and when the Fourth of July rolled around, we celebrated with our biggest party of the year. These were afternoons of heat and laughter, of sun on my skin and the smell of all-American hot dogs and hamburgers on the grill. At night, fireworks lit the sky, shouting our love of country for the whole city to see.

I lived a childhood of endless sun, palm trees and gentle breezes, yet still, I had nightmares of apocalypse, which remain with me now. At five, my mother and I stand on the moon as we watch the blue globe of the earth explode into millions of jagged bits. The dark sky turns white as letters from earth descend upon us like snow, turning the moon's darkness bright. In elementary school, aliens invade every night when I close my eyes. One by one, they transform my classmates into complacently happy beings with rubbery limbs and smiling, vacant faces. I do not know whom to trust and the air is thick with eerie fear. In college, it is a nuclear end to the world that fills my dreams. Sirens sound as warning lights flash. I flee for life down narrow corridors as tidal waves of water rush behind me.

Dreams are my honest mirror. They know no pretense and succumb to no lies. My dreams of apocalypse are among my earliest memories, so much a part of me that they are like an old friend. Now, as childhood grows distant, they are only occasional visitors. When they do come, I awaken in fear but with a sense of comfort that comes with familiarity. Yes, here you are again. It's been a long time.

—⟋⟍—

I was well into my thirties when I realized that not everyone dreams of the end of the world, and almost forty before I finally knew why I have such dreams.

I was in Shanghai with my father as part of a tour, one of those that now departs daily from Monterey Park in Los Angeles. Thousands who left frightened and fleeing after the Communist Revolution in 1949, now return to China in the safety of tour groups, traveling the homeland in air-conditioned buses, sleeping safely in Sheratons and Hiltons. Last year my father and I took a cruise up the Yangze River. My mother, her memories of war still too fresh after nearly fifty years, stayed home.

In Shanghai, the evening before the cruise, my father and I walked along the riverfront Bund, a walkway overlooking the mouth of the Yangze as it yawns into the Pacific. Grand art deco buildings glowed in the early evening, reflected in the waters of the river. My father was struck by the mood of the street, which was crowded with people leisurely strolling, taking in the view, happy and laughing. Many enjoyed popsicles that looked like giant orange tires on a stick filled with white frozen cream. At an intersection, we could see the dense life of Nanjing Dong Street, which was lit brightly with neon signs. Shops were open and people walked out with bags of new clothing, linens and school supplies for their children. Restaurants were noisy with business, serving Chinese and European food.

When we walked past the Bank of China building, I asked my father to stop, and I pulled out my camera. Just after graduating from National Central University, Dad worked on the third floor of this decoratively European building, rendered in stone and wrought iron. He helped to control sugar prices that were spiraling out of sight. He was a young man then, his black hair so thick that barbers complained it dulled their scissors. Now, his hair is peppered gray and sparse.

"The last time I was on the Yangze River, it was fifty years ago and it was *tao nan*," my father said. *Tao nan*, a phrase that to me is as old as the words "Mama" and "Baba." *Tao nan* means to flee disaster, to fight for life.

I am hungry for my father's memory, famished for the past that is my own. Amid the bleaching light of Los Angeles, I have lost my way. I seek my history, even if it is full of fire.

—ɯ—

The famed Cathay Hotel is next door to the Bank of China, but even so, my father said he never went inside. He passed its windows every evening, hearing the sounds of Americans and Europeans laughing and talking, happily lubricated at the bar, dining on China's fine dishes and throwing away leftovers. On the street outside the Cathay, those with brown and blond hair wore thick coats and warm leather shoes. Those with black hair wore torn clothes that hardly kept them warm in winter. Some slept beneath store windows that displayed the finest of European hats and coats on Nanjing Dong Street.

"The nationalist government was corrupt," my father said. "They sold our country to foreigners." Inflation was out of control, and the Chinese people struggled to have enough to eat. Even my father had nothing but *man tou*, steamed bread of flour and water, for breakfast, lunch and dinner. He could feel revolution in air that grew thick with fear. The Communists were coming, overtaking cities one by one, making their way to Shanghai. They had already invaded the village where he was born in Shandong Province. Full of anger from years of poverty and corrupt abuses, they humiliated and killed anyone who opposed them. My father told me that his uncle stood watching as they buried his parents alive.

It was where we stood on the Bund that my father first contemplated leaving China, the only world his family had ever known. The timing would have to be just right as even one day could mean the difference between life or death. He would acquire silver coins that could hold value wherever he went. He would let no one know. Fifty years later, standing on a now bustling Bund, I could still see the fear in his face.

—ɯ—

That night, sleeping safely in the high-rise Shanghai JC Mandarin Hotel, my dreams returned. A spaceship hovers over Central Avenue in Albuquerque, sending down a pinpoint beam of bright light that splits a building in two. The invasion begins again. Every molecule of my body becomes alert and aware, poised for survival, ready to flee before it is too late.

When I awoke, I realized for the first time why apocalypse comes to me in my sleep.

"Dad," I said in the morning. "You know how Mom always dreams of *tao nan*? Well, I always dream of *tao nan*, too."

"But how can you?" he asked.

When I explained, I saw disappointment shadow his face. He had done everything that he could to shield me, to give me some other kind of life than the one he had known. He had raised me in southern California, bought me blue jeans and a new car when I was a teenager, sent me to the best American schools. But I grew up knowing *tao nan*, anyway.

—⧄—

In Albuqureque, the air grows cool. Soon flame-colored leaves from the tree outside the window will scatter all over the city, onto roads and parking lots. Like an autumn wind, war scatters souls. My family arose from the soil of the Yellow River and never wandered far from it. Now they live amid bright lights and shiny cars in Los Angeles. In New York that September day, thousands of souls in dust and ash were scattered. They drifted past Chinese restaurants along Mott Street, past the windows full of pastry in Little Italy. They were blown uptown, where they caressed the spire of the Empire State Building. They floated over the waterways, away from a city that now, too, knows smoke and fire.

SKIN

by Rahna Reiko Rizzuto

I

Who am I if not my mother's daughter? Snub-nosed. Freckled. Enemy to her country. Your enemy, by skin, once there is a war. Interned—in a camp, in the prairie, behind barbed wire, at a racetrack, with only what she could carry. With guns pointing at her; guards with machine guns pointing at her, or were they only rifles? Perhaps only rifles, but in any case with searchlights and curfews and rules that say you cannot congregate, you cannot speak that foreign language. Good for her that she could not speak that foreign language. She could not speak at all—no words in the mouth of a baby three months old, four months, one year, two. With Shirley Temple curls, watching the tumbleweeds dance from her grandmother's arms; learning to crawl on bricks laid over dirt because there is no floor. She was imprisoned with one hundred and ten thousand other American children and their immigrant parents, in sixteen American assembly centers, in ten American camps. I say: innocents. You say: inscrutable, untrustworthy, "particularly repulsive... to the civilian population." How can we say, now, among the children and the old folks, the Americans and the people who were not allowed to become naturalized, if there were spies? My mother was lucky. She was too young to be the boy who was beaten, with pistols, bats and rifles, to be housed in the "bull pen" outdoors in the middle of winter, to be placed in the stockade and left for dead. My mother has no scars, except the ones that we all carry. The question of "who am I?" against the flinch of: enemy. She can shun the culture, the food, the language.

But she cannot change her skin.

Your enemy's daughter is also your enemy. And your enemy was a zealot, who would turn a man into a bomb. Turn a plane into a bomb. Put a sixteen-year-old boy into a plane and send him on the sacred wind, on a prayer to save his mother, on a path to glory, because his leader says go; his leader is divine. Who would send him into a ship, into a plane, into a military installation with a "*banzai!*" and a last wish, winking out, that his mother might again eat clean, unadulterated white rice instead of husks and stems and leaves. That his mother will not be one of those who dies from malnutrition because the children needed food. This boy is related to me, though my family has lost him; his mother, too—we don't know her name, or where she lives— it's been more than one hundred years of silence and forgetting since my ancestors came to America. But she is your enemy, my unmet, distant cousin. Look for her among the women who join community exercises to defend their honor with a stick of sharp bamboo, to pass buckets of water from the well to a burning building. A single building. She is standing, at the munitions factory, on the night shift, sleeping in front of a conveyor belt, in front of the machine that cannot make bullets because there is no metal left.

She is saying goodbye to her son.

II

I am the niece, too, of my great uncle. He of jaunty step. Quick smile. Hero to his country. An enlisted man, a soldier in Hawaii when Pearl Harbor is bombed, a boy who scrambles beneath the attack and then immediately reports for duty. You say: enemy and you discharge him. I say: third-generation American, son of a World War I vet. A young man who does not give up when they take away his gun; he digs ditches, he volunteers, he agitates to rejoin, to be one of those island boys age sixteen to more than fifty who volunteer to form their own battalion and then their own regiment, all Americans of *banzai* blood. He crawls through the mud in

Mississippi, fights the mosquitoes that bite through his clothes while his brother is being held in an internment camp because they share enemy eyes, enemy skin; but this one—in the right place at the right time—he is your savior. He proves his ability to follow orders; his desire to save the world; his loyalty. My great uncle will break codes in the Pacific for the military because he knows the language, and my great uncle will serve on the front lines when he is old enough, to replace those who don't survive. You say: soldiers should die for their country. I hear: "send them in so we don't have to deal with their offspring." These are ones who fight, and die, and believe.

The kamikazes who win.

Your savior's niece is also your savior. But your savior has been in a ditch for days in the freezing rain somewhere in France. He has taken a hill, lost a hill, taken it again. He has lost friends, watched them die; he has observed them from the inside, where they are soft and sloppy, when it would be much easier to scoop the pieces up with a spoon than to imagine where they once fit. If he had a spoon. He has heard the death laugh; the death rattle; the death sob; the death silence; the death thud. "*Itai, itai*"—it hurts—in the forest. Your savior follows orders even when there are only ten men left in his company, when the commander stays behind but he must move in to rescue the men from Texas who are cut off. Two hundred men. This is the Lost Battalion; he will save them, he and one of the most deco- rated units in World War II, he and 800 other casualties. Four for every man saved. He will be called "fanatic" by *Time* magazine. He will be called crazy, a "little brown soldier" in a hellish forest. He will break through lines that even tanks could not break through, and he will be injured, my great-uncle. He will joke, despite his wounds. And when he sees the missing limbs around him, he will shake down his thermometer when the nurse isn't looking so that his fellow soldiers get care first. He will not see the infection growing in the shrapnel in his back. My uncle will die for you—for us—in a hospital in America.

And his parents—American citizens—won't be allowed to leave Hawaii for his funeral.

III

I am, as my family tightens, the niece of my great-aunt. A young American woman, interned with the rest, but that is all behind her now. Once you restore her rights and her citizenship, she joins the Allied Occupation to help you rebuild the enemy country, and so she is your witness both in America and Japan. When she reaches the ruined city, you deliver her to work by bus since there is nowhere to live in the rubble. No buildings left standing for thirteen square miles. And still, this is the adventure of her lifetime, her chance to help. She goes with your doctor to the homes of mothers who have given birth to stillborn babies; she is your translator as that woman invites you in, hoping for any small help or kindness you can give. In a room at the Red Cross Hospital, which was bent and cracked but is still partially standing, my great-aunt tallies statistics, in long addition, on radiation poisoning in human beings who are studied carefully by American doctors but not treated. She thinks: this information will put an end to this terrible weapon. You think: we have a winner here. We know where the enemy was standing, what sheltered them, whether they were facing toward or away, how long it took them to get out, whether they jumped into the river, dodged the fire, were lucky enough to have the maggots picked out of their wounds. We have the body of the dead baby, its blood, its skin, but we have no cure for them. No advice, no warnings; we are not looking for solutions but for evidence of our force. One hundred thousand dead to save American lives, one hundred thousand more dying at different rates, from different causes, and we need to know how, and why, and where, to protect ourselves from retaliation.

Because there will be, always is, a response.

The niece of your witness can tell the story. Must feel her anger, follow it to Hiroshima to discover what my great-aunt was not allowed to see: the child trying to fit her mother's eye back into its socket. The schoolboy whose face has melted — no eyes, nose, lips, ears, no skin. I am looking for war, trying to understand my family, I am interviewing the enemy, and they tell me: It was dark; I was blown back ten meters; everything was flat; they were walking like ghosts, their hands in front of them; their skin hung like rags; they were crying for water. They were crying "Help me," "*Itai*," "It hurts." The whole city was silent, a city of ashes and not a single sound. It was black; it was red; everything was gray and hot, so hot; it was beautiful. A young woman tells me how white the bones at her feet were, the ones in what used to be her living room, and how they gleamed in the sun. I am telling you how she described them.

Her mother's bones.

IV

I am the mother of the targets. My two sons, dark blond, blue eyed; they are Japanese, Chinese, Italian, Irish, English, German and French. They are five and three, Americans, and they are in school when my husband sees the first plane, too low, through his car windshield, and calls home from the Brooklyn Bridge to say: Go get them. Take them out of school. I am in Hiroshima when he dials his cell phone; I am not there to take their hands, dodge the documents and the fiberglass falling in the schoolyard, bring them back to our home, less than a kilometer away from the fallen buildings, within the radius that was instant death for the first atomic bomb. They call me with the news on this September morning—one ground zero to another; too much and not enough distance in between—and they tell me: "Mommy, a plane flew into the towers and broke them down. There is paper all over the sky. It is very sad." They do not know of the thousands of people who were trapped in the rubble in Hiroshima surrounded by firestorms after the bomb itself had fallen; of the thousands in America who were hijacked in the air, or trapped in elevators or in their offices, with the full knowledge that there was no escape, that they were dying, that there was not enough time. They do not know of the people who jumped. I assure them: "Everything will be okay. You are safe." You assure us: "We can protect ourselves by bombing someone else's country. We can protect ourselves by rounding up our enemies and holding them for a period of indefinite time." Both of us lying. We are trading lives, losing lives, labeling them, never even seeing them. If there is one thing I am sure of—a conviction that carries no hope, and no protection—it is this: No one has the right to kill my sons.

RAHNA REIKO RIZZUTO

Targets are small, human, fragile; this is how they die: Shot in the back. Stitched through the middle by machine guns. Melted. Ceasing in the womb. Ignited by airplane fuel. Vomiting. Veins bursting through the skin in purple blotches, hearts bursting, brains exploding on the pavement from one hundred stories high. They cry for their mothers, they search for their children, they throw themselves on their little brothers, they never find their way home. These visions are my mother's gift to me, the bequests of my friend-and-enemy family, the spoils of my excavation of the many roots of war. But the truth that I was looking for didn't come from the past; it came from my children. They tell me that, if it is skin we are aiming at—skin, eyes, shape of the eyes, cheekbones, stature, shape of the nose— then it is skin we will see: How a mother raises her son's swollen face toward the kettle of precious water. Just as you or I would do, trying to help our injured child. Never imagining that the skin of his lips will attach to it, the skin of his lips will slide off; the skin of his face burnt, irradiated, that his lips will pull away from the hole where his mouth is. His skin, no longer useful, no longer human.

That his lips will come off, on the spout, when he falls.

The Karen

The Karen people, the largest of Burma's ethnic hill tribes,
live in the eastern mountains of Burma.

THE KAREN PEOPLE

by Dang Ngo

Displaced People

The Karen people, along with most other people in Burma, have long suffered at the hands of the Burmese military regime, called the State Peace and Development Council (S.P.D.C.). This regime has been widely condemned by international human rights groups, governments, and the United States for their pervasive violations of human rights. Anywhere from two to four million people are internally displaced in Burma, at least one million of these in the ethnic nationality areas, surviving or hiding in the forests or as beggars in the towns.

DANG NGO

Rice for Life

The Karen traditionally live in remote villages as rice farmers. December marks the beginning of the dry season and rice harvest in Burma. This is also when the S.P.D.C. are most active. As part of their "4-cuts" strategy to cut off food, funds, recruits and intelligence to the opposition, the S.P.D.C. enter hill tribe villages and often kill, torture, steal, or demand labor from villagers. They also destroy crops and livestock, ruining the community's capacity to sustain themselves.

Living on the Edge
Already weakened by malaria and other diseases,
many people die, especially children and the elderly.

DANG NGO

Cause and Effect

These are landmines of the Burmese Military. Often, they are planted on popular trails or at the base of peoples' homes to maim and terrorize them. The use of land-mines along the border of Burma is pervasive. The Burmese military use landmines not only to kill and injure soldiers but to deter villagers from coming back to their villages, and to kill livestock.

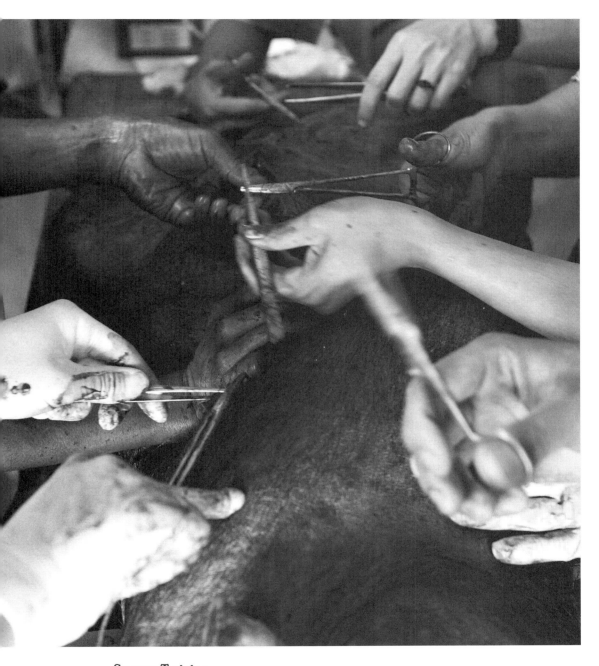

Surgery Training
Karen medic students practice their surgical skills on a pig at
Dr. Cynthia's Mae Tao Clinic in Mae Sot, Thailand.

DANG NGO

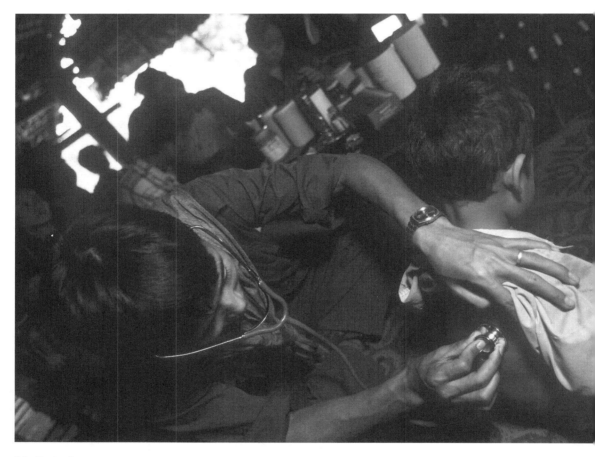

Medic in Action

At extreme risk to himself, Johnny Htoo, a backpack medic, treks from village to village throughout the jungles of Burma to administer medicine to villagers. Most of the villages he reaches have not seen a doctor in years.

Recovery
A patient recovers in a field clinic after stepping on a landmine
in the Paan District of Karen State, Burma.

DANG NGO

Child Soldier

When this boy was six, his parents and brother were murdered in their village by the S.P.D.C. Now twelve years old, he fights off the S.P.D.C. with the Karen National Liberation Army. There are an estimated 300,000 child soldiers around the world today. In Burma, this is often the result of the severe oppression of the hill tribe people, who often face the choice of slavery, living in hiding, or resisting.

Tragedy
Naw Eh Nah and her baby examine the remains of their home which was attacked and burnt down by the S.P.D.C. Nah, twenty-two years old, became a widow one month earlier when her husband stepped on an S.P.D.C. landmine.

DANG NGO

Giving Life

Life is nourished amid war. The "longneck" Karen, often termed the "Padaung,"
suffer as much as any other Karen.

Agility

Retaining Spirituality

The Burmese military's partner in crime, the Democratic Buddhist Karen Army
(D.K.B.A.), burnt down all the homes in this village and then demanded the monks
leave so they could also burn the monastery. The monks refused and said they would
rather perish in their spiritual home. Remembering their own Buddhist background,
the D.K.B.A. ultimately decided to leave the monastery alone.

LEGENDS

The author's father, on his wedding day.

WITHOUT ANGER

by Shymala Dason

The members of my family who lived through the Japanese Occupation of Malaya often reminisced with eagerness and laughter—even when they were describing soldiers cutting off the heads of civilians in the streets. As a small child, I thought war meant not having to go to school and having lots of people around the table at each meal. I thought war was a kind of party. Old enough to know better now, I wonder how they are able to laugh at all.

June, July 1941: Western powers cut Japan off from oil and other resources needed for the war effort; Southeast Asia and the East Indies have these in abundant supply. Japan acquires bases in southern Indochina.

My father was a twenty-four-year-old lab assistant when the bombs, air-raid drills, dead bodies and fear came to Malaya. He became an air-raid warden, happily volunteering for the Air Raid Patrol (A.R.P.) under the British. Japanese bombers might any minute fill the sky, but the Union Jack still flew in front of government buildings. His friend, a young, Malayan-born Japanese who had been a lodger with my father's family was taken away to India and interned by British authorities.

December 8, 1941: Japanese bomb Manila. War is declared. The Japanese invade Malaya, landing in the north. British resistance is a shambles. Japanese troops pour down the peninsula. The British evacuate. Malaya and Malayans — Malay, Chinese, Indian — are on their own.

Daddy stayed in the A.R.P. after the British abandoned Malaya. Japanese bombs were still falling. His family was poor and couldn't afford a bomb shelter. They lived in an old-fashioned, wooden house with a coconut-thatch roof, raised on cement pilings. When the bombs fell, the family hid under the house with the chickens.

January 11, 1942: Japanese forces reach Kuala Lumpur. The Rising Sun replaces the Union Jack.

My father went from the A.R.P. to being a translator under the Japanese, a more dangerous job. The Occupation forces were a different breed than his long-time friend; these Japanese decapitated those who didn't bow fast enough or hand over their property with sufficient cheerfulness. He and the other translators lied to the Japanese, feeding information to their own people right under the noses of the Japanese. They spoke quickly or in dialect, gambling that the invaders would not understand enough to realize what they were doing.

When I was a child, there was a mass World War II graveyard underneath a field near our house in Kuala Lumpur. I played in it — all the children in the neighborhood did, though we were told not to. I used to imagine the bones underneath, trying to see their shapes in the little protrusions and dips.

Many people did not work during the first year of the Occupation; people who went to work or school sometimes didn't make it home. Daddy's family was too poor for him to have that option. I also like to think that he was too brave. I can hear him giving his big laugh and saying, "Why should they do anything to me? I never did anything to anybody!" as he went out the door with his brisk, solid step down the wooden stairs, past the poultry, out the mud lane and into the main street.

These were difficult times. The Japanese placed decapitated heads on main streets everywhere as a "teaching aid." My father's younger brother died of typhoid coupled with a wartime lack of medicine. When Daddy talked about it, he did so sadly but without anger. He said what a good, gentle man Uncle John was. "What to do? That was those days, how it was. What to do." He never blamed the Japanese or hated them; he only hated war. When his Malayan-Japanese friend was released from internment, my father's family welcomed him back into their home.

—⁂—

My father's stories were all a kind of fairy tale to me. The father I knew was a big, laughing man who liked nothing better than to indulge in the Malaysian national obsession of searching for the latest and best snack food, an obsession he raised to an art form. Yet he was frightened of dogs, bicycles and motorbikes. As a teenager I joked that he must have used up all his courage during the war.

—⁂—

Across town, my mother's family had a different approach to coping with the war. She was fourteen when the Occupation began. Her father, Thatha, was an anti-malarial engineer with the Public Works Department and had money for an air-raid shelter and easy access to labor and materials. Thatha didn't join the A.R.P. He didn't even work for more than six months; he couldn't stand seeing the heads in the street. But he had his own kind of courage.

Within three days of the bombing of Manila, the family valuables were buried under a layer of wood and cement in the middle of the living room floor, safe from war. Hearing the stories of rapes and brutalities, Thatha rearranged the furniture inside his house, setting the big, old-fashioned cupboards at angles so his skinny teenaged girls could squeeze behind them in hiding. He planted extra vegetables in the garden, raised some goats, got several young single men to move in with his

SHYMALA DASON

family and pretend to be his sons, brought in his two married daughters and their families, and kept them all safe. As best he could, he also cared for his laborers and their families. He treated them with such care that when he died three decades after the war, they were there to see him laid to rest.

My mother was formed during the Occupation. While hiding behind cupboards in the warm, stuffy darkness and not daring to take more than shallow breaths, she learned that she was supposed to be afraid, that she was never to show herself directly. She tried very hard to teach me the same thing.

My mother often recalled her maternal grandfather, a man so proud he voluntarily starved to death during the war. The family was never short of food. They supplied their neighbors with vegetables, and once a week my grandmother would butcher a goat and sell the meat. Twenty people ate at their table, laden with tapioca and sweet potatoes—boiled and then fried—with chili and peanuts. But because it wasn't first-quality Basmati rice, my great-grandfather simply refused to eat. My mother told this story whenever she wanted someone to feel like dirt. To die from sheer pride implied a higher standard than I could ever hope to achieve.

At first I thought the stories colorful. Later I wanted to get as far away as I could from these values, frozen in time since World War II and non-negotiable because an old man had been too stubborn and too stupid to stay alive. That's how I wound up in America.

1945: Hiroshima and Nagasaki are bombed. Japan surrenders Malaya to the British. Japanese forces are ordered home.

My father had married my mother's elder sister a few years earlier, and she was now carrying their second child. She painted a Union Jack and hung it on the house the day before the British officially took over. It was a risk, but she was strong-willed, pregnant and euphoric. They put up the flag. My second sister was born that night; the next morning, my aunt died. My father's brothers climbed up the front of the house and tore down the flag she had raised. No one could bear to see it.

In 1946, my parents married.

As a child, I sat on the floor and listened as my elders painted word pictures. I never knew how much was embroidered by the joy of storytelling. I tried to see what had really happened through their words.

I didn't understand their world until September 11. Suddenly, there were military jets flying over my sleepy Maryland suburb. We wept, we mourned, we raged, we struggled to understand, our hearts crying for safety. Finally, I could understand my parents' time. I understood my mother's fear. And I saw that I had to understand my father's laughter and that I had to remember that no matter what horrors were in the wind, it also bore sweet scents. And that there were bright stars overhead.

"Chairman Mao Enjoys Swimming in the Yangtze,"
The People's Daily. (1966)

The author's sister, Xu Ruo-Dan, poses next to
Mao's statue in 1968.

DEATH OF A RED GUARD

by Xujun Eberlein

The obvious association between these two black-and-white photographs is, of course, the appearance of Chairman Mao. The first one, with Mao in a bathrobe waving to us from a boat, records an historical day, July 16, 1966. I first saw this photo on the front page of China's most authoritative newspaper, *The People's Daily,* under the headline "Chairman Mao Enjoys Swimming in Yangze." At the age of seventy-three, Mao had swum fifteen kilometers across the world's second largest river. I, like all the kids in my elementary class, cheered for our great leader's health, unaware of the ultimatum it sent to his political enemies signaling the start of the Cultural Revolution. Soon practically everything was regarded as the "four olds"— old thought, old culture, old tradition and old custom—and had to be denounced and purged from Chinese society. Within a few short months the Red Guard movement, started by some middle school students in Beijing, washed over China with the force of a tidal wave.

In the second photo, Mao, this time a life-size statue in the background, is again waving. In front, a teenage girl wearing a Red Guard uniform and armband is holding Mao's book, her braided pigtails stretching out like two brushes. This photo was taken two years later, in the week before July 16; its exact date and photographer can no longer be traced. It was taken from a low angle, as the girl's right arm with the book is exaggerated, making her look like a figure from a revolutionary poster.

It is no coincidence that these two photos are both in my album. The teenage Red Guard is my big sister, Ruo-Dan. She was sixteen. Each time I stare at the two photos, I see the connection between them that others can't.

—⟋⟍—

The hot wind in July 1968 blew across Chongqing, the largest industrial city in southern China. In the chaos of the Cultural Revolution, the Red Guards had split into two factions. Led by school youths, the adults split into separate factions as well, each faction fervently claiming to possess the "true" revolutionary line of Mao and viewing the opposition as villains. Both sides pledged to fight to the death for Chairman Mao. Armed fights, *wu dou*, between the two factions had been going on for almost two years and had escalated to new heights. The noise kept me awake at night. Machine guns, artillery pieces and tanks were no longer just an unreal scene from war movies.

Mother, as a primary school principal, had little to do after all the schools were closed by the Red Guards. She spent most of her time at home. Before the split into factions, she had been subjected to numerous denunciations by her young students. Now, with the other faction to confront, the youngsters lost interest and left my mother alone. Worried over the armed fights, Mother sent two of my sisters to hide in Grandma's home village several hundred miles down the Yangze; she prohibited me, her third daughter, from wandering the streets. But she did not know how to protect her oldest daughter, Ruo-Dan, a Red Guard leader in the Third Middle School. Our house had no telephone; even had we access to one, there was not a phone number in Ruo-Dan's school we could reach. Mother could have taken a one-hour bus ride to the school, but Ruo-Dan certainly wouldn't have been happy about that. She and Mother were in opposite factions—in those days everyone I knew, be it housewife or pre-teen, was in one of the two factions.

The earliest and most radical Red Guard faction in the city was named "8.15" because it was started by a group of students at Chongqing University on August 15, 1966. Ruo-Dan's middle school was near the university, so she joined this faction. Perhaps ironically, the government institute my father once headed consisted of older

people who were also in the 8.15 faction. These people were more interested in perse-
cuting my father than in attacking the opposing faction. Each day Father went to his
office to receive denunciations from this "revolutionary mass"—his former subordi-
nates. Unlike Ruo-Dan, I had the misfortune to witness the 8.15 faction humiliate
our parents by forcing them to wear dunce caps at public rallies. Once the opposing
faction was formed, it was natural for my parents—and me—to choose it. Strangely,
my young brain could not make the connection between the "8.15" at Father's institute and the one at my sister's school. Ruo-Dan's factional stand never bothered me
very much.

Ruo-Dan visited us at home on weekends, but I hadn't seen her for several
weeks. I missed her; she was my hero and protector. So when her tanned oval face
finally appeared on a mid-July Saturday night, I was overjoyed. For the entire Sunday
I was a shadow to her body, while she avoided being alone with Mother. She showed
me a sword dance she had recently learned. She showed me how to jump up onto a
table while keeping both feet together. I could do none of these things—just like
I could not wear her Red Guard armband no matter how much I wanted.

When the night curtain fell and she was about to leave again, I asked her keenly,
"Are you going to be back next Saturday?"

"I'll see," she said. "Oh yes! I have pictures to show you! I just took an entire roll
last week, but it will not be developed until Monday."

My eyes widened. How could she take an entire roll of pictures? The only way
I knew pictures could be taken was one at a time—by sitting on a bench in a photo
studio.

"My troop has a 135-mm hand camera now," she added proudly. "I got to play
with it because of my position." I was going to ask if she could bring the new toy
home next week, when Mother interrupted.

"Little Jia, with all this shooting going on, perhaps you should stay home,"
she said.

Mother always called Ruo-Dan by her baby name, given because of her birth on
the bank of the Jia-Ling River. Mother's worry was not ill-founded. A factory field
near their school had turned into a battlefield. A close comrade and schoolmate of

Ruo-Dan's, Ai Shu-Quan, had been killed by a bullet from the opposite faction. He was a leader of the armed fighting group called Fishing Boat. Ruo-Dan and her friends buried him in the Red Guard Martyrs Cemetery in Sha'ping Park. They had vowed in front of his grave to carry forward his unfulfilled wish and take the Cultural Revolution to the end. Each of them scooped up a handful of earth to cover his coffin. The hardest thing, my sister told me afterward, was watching Ai Shu-Quan's parents and siblings crying.

Ruo-Dan cut Mother short. "Ma, don't worry about it. I'm not in the armed fighting group. I can't stay home just because there's danger at school; all my comrades are there."

We were all silent for a few moments. Then Mother said, "Be very careful." I walked with Ruo-Dan to the No. 2 bus line. On the way she asked if I remembered Chairman Mao's instruction, "Go into the big rivers to be tempered."

I nodded.

"Big rivers don't have to be real rivers, you know?" she said.

I nodded again and said I understood that big rivers were also a metaphor for revolutionary practice. She looked satisfied with my answer. I waved to her as the bus pulled out and tried to tell myself a week of time really wasn't that hard to pass.

—⟋⟍—

Two days later it was Tuesday, July 16, the second anniversary of Chairman Mao's famous swim in the Yangze, but I did not remember that. Those days I had found a way to entertain myself that all the neighborhood kids, especially girls, enjoyed tremendously. Kids can always find entertainment, even in such a revolutionary storm. With the same fanaticism with which we had collected Chairman Mao's photo buttons a year before, we now made, collected and traded paper-cuts of revolutionary heroes. Neighborhood kids went to stationery stores and bought different colors of cheap waxed paper. We traced paper-cut patterns on the backside of square waxed paper with a pencil, placed the traced pattern on a wooden board and carefully cut along the pattern's lines with a woodcutting knife. Then we would show off our collections to each other and compete. The one who collected the most patterns got the biggest admiration regardless of her parents' faction allegiance. I was thinking that I would become the one who had the biggest collection of paper-cut arts in the world. That Tuesday noon I did not take a nap, as I was concentrating on making a paper-cut of a scene in a revolutionary model ballet, Red Women Soldiers. I did not know that fifteen miles away, Ruo-Dan did not take a nap either. Unlike me, she solidly remembered the day's revolutionary importance.

—⁓—

Ruo-Dan had proposed a commemorative swim on this special day. She and her fellow Red Guard friends planned to go right after lunch. The walk from the school to the Jia-Ling River would take about half an hour and would warm them up before they jumped into the cold water. It was a peaceful noon in the Third Middle School. No gunfire had been heard since the previous week's deadly battle in a nearby factory, a victory for the 8.15 faction. Now there were only the sparse chirps of cicadas under bright summer sun. In the dining hall the middle school students had lunch together, and the practical boys said they would swim after their noon siesta. It's not good to move a lot right after finishing a meal, they argued; after a two-hour nap, everyone would have fresh spirit for this revolutionary activity—and by then it wouldn't be so hot for the walk.

But Ruo-Dan had no patience for such excuses. She surely could skip a nap on such a special day! Her heart had been set on this meaningful action. Since Chairman Mao's call to Chinese youth to "go into the big rivers to be tempered," she had been learning to swim in the school's pool, but the pool was child's play compared to big rivers. What would be more meaningful than to go into a river for the first time today to prove her determination?

It did not take much for Ruo-Dan to convince her three roommates. After all, they had swum in pools before. Why did they have to wait for the boys?

The four girls walked out of the schoolyard filled with daring and vigor, red silk bands on their left arms, faded green People's Liberation Army uniforms covering their swimming suits. They crossed the sleepy streets, taking a shortcut through the Architecture College campus and out onto the trail down to the riverside. They walked past vegetable fields, barren hills and a factory, at last approaching the bank of the river. A gust of cold, moist air pushed into their faces, supplanting the day's heat as the immense river came into view.

It looked different. The surface was much wider. There were no boats. The usually clear and calm current was muddy and swift. Broken tree branches and tangled vegetation swirled past. Even the inexperienced eyes of these sixteen-year-old girls could tell that the water was rising. A big rock the boys used to jump off of had almost disappeared under the water. The waves washing upward along the dirt bank did not look kind and fun.

The girls surveyed the bank, trying to find a nice spot to enter the water. A small inlet, where tips of long grasses could be seen waving in the water, looked calmer. Ruo-Dan decided that was the place, and the others agreed. They took off their shoes. They took off their P.L.A. uniforms. They looked at each other; no one made a move.

Ruo-Dan read hesitation in her friends' eyes. She was a leader. A leader should always be at the head of her people.

"All right, " she said, "I'll go first. I am going to measure the water's depth and signal you. OK?"

"Perhaps we should wait for them," one girl said with an unsure tone.

"No," Ruo-Dan responded.

Later, I would try again and again to guess what had being going on in her mind at that moment. For some reason, among the hundreds of Chairman Mao's quotations that I could recite, this was the one that kept echoing in my ear: "Be resolute, fear no sacrifice and surmount ten-thousand difficulties to win victory." A famous musician even made this quotation a song, and it was the song broadcast over loudspeakers by both factions in every armed fight. Whenever we heard this song we would run inside and close the doors tightly.

Was this the music playing in Ruo-Dan's head when she walked into the river without another word? In a blink her entire body sank into the water, her shoulder-length black hair floating behind her.

The other girls watched Ruo-Dan's black hair fade in and out of the water a few times. The water was taking her away fast—faster than they'd prepared for.

Soon there was no sign of anything but the brown-yellow waves.

The girls waited. They waited for Ruo-Dan's face to spring out the water again and signal to them. They waited until panic finally set in.

"She's gone!" one girl burst out. As if on command, all three of them started to cry. They sat on the dirt of the bank, screaming "Xu Ruo-Dan!" again and again. The riverside was empty. No one heard their cries.

Half an hour later, exhausted with crying, the girls finally got up and left the river along the same path that Ruo-Dan had led them earlier. They staggered all the way back to school like drunks. Not until another half hour had passed did the others, just up from their nap, hear the shocking news. A frantic crowd ran to the river.

"Did you call the workers in the factory?" a boy shouted at the numb girls.

The girls' vacant expression told him that no such possibility had crossed their minds.

Since the start of the Cultural Revolution, classes had been suspended and there were only student Red Guards in the school. The boys pleaded with the riverside factory workers for help; they were in the same faction. Hundreds of men and teenagers spent the rest of the afternoon searching in the water and along the river-bank for any sign of Ruo-Dan. Night fell. They did not find her that day.

The search continued early next morning. Around ten, they found her body under water only a few hundred meters from where she had gone in. Grasses were tightly wound around one of her feet, preventing her from floating up or being washed away. She looked as if she were sleeping.

My parents received notice soon after the body was discovered and immediately rushed to Ruo-Dan's school, leaving me home alone with no instructions. The next morning, as soon as I opened my eyes from a confused night of strange dreams, I got up and walked to the bus station where I had seen Ruo-Dan off four days before. I waited in the line for a long time to get on a bus. The crowded bus took more than an hour to arrive at Sha'ping terminal. I was not crying. I hadn't cried since I heard of Ruo-Dan's death the day before.

I ran across the dusty suburban street through the gate of the Third Middle School, once the best school in Chongqing. Inside the gate I ran directly toward the statue of Chairman Mao. At the statue I turned right into a three-story building. In the second-floor meeting room, I saw my parents sitting silently, surrounded by a crowd of teenage girls and boys. Mother's eyes were swollen like walnuts. When I appeared at the door, my parents stared like they didn't see me. There was no motion in their faces or bodies. I looked around fiercely but did not see Ruo-Dan's body anywhere.

"Where is my big sister?" I demanded loudly.

One of Ruo-Dan's close comrades pulled me out to the hallway and whispered that Ruo-Dan had already been buried the previous afternoon.

"No!" I screamed. "Where is her grave? Take me there! I want to see her! I want to see her!"

The girl started to weep and did not answer me. I charged into the meeting room again and shouted to Mother: "I want to see Big Sister! Take me to see her!"

Father responded in a low roar: "Stop it! Your mother hasn't slept the whole night! Don't make her cry again!"

Then I heard Mother's trembling voice. "Third, my third, your sister's coffin has been nailed," she said. "You can't see her any more." Her last few words were lost in sobs.

"I am going to pry the coffin open!" I said firmly.

Ruo-Dan's friend looked into my eyes. "Little sister," she said with an earnest tone I'd never heard from anyone before. "Your sister is a hero. If I could exchange my life for hers, I would rather die myself."

I looked up to the sincere red eyes of these big sisters and brothers around me and finally cried with all the tears a twelve-year-old girl could have. Not until much later did it cross my mind that all of these middle school students, my sister's comrades, were in the opposite faction from my parents and me.

That day, I got the prints from my sister's final pictures. There she was with Chairman Mao's statue.

—⁓—

Mother went half insane after Ruo-Dan's death. She would sit, empty eyed, and repeatedly chatter, "I shouldn't have named her 'Little Jia'…then the Jia-Ling River wouldn't have taken her back…"

Or she would say with a blind smile, "What a strong child, like a calf," as if her little Jia were still alive.

She kept all the windows in the house open, day and night. If I wanted to close them, Mother would scold me: "Stop! How can your sister find a way to get back inside?!"

My sister's comrades buried Ruo-Dan in the nearby backyard of the Normal School of Chongqing, on a small hill next to a stream. The stream served as the border dividing the Normal School and a farm area. Near the grave, a wooden bridge crossed the stream. Two weeks after Ruo-Dan's death, her comrades came to tell Mother that they were going to move her to the Sha'ping Park Martyrs Cemetery. This somehow comforted Mother. She waited and waited; her life seemed to gain more meaning in the waiting. But it never happened. Year after year, I went to that lone dirt tomb with Mother on every single birthday of Ruo-Dan's, until my young heart could no longer fight the current of Mother's endless tears. I stopped going. Coincidentally or not, the armed fights ended after my sister's death. In late July of that year, after quietly watching the Red Guards' armed fights across all of China for almost two years, after numerous solemn and heroic sacrifices on his behalf, Chairman Mao finally stepped in and harshly ordered both factions to cease fire. The great leader's order was promptly carried out. In November, two men who had been commanding Chongqing's armed fights, one from each faction, were jailed. As "heroes" turned to criminals, history was inverted once again. The Red Guards who had been killed in the skirmishes were no longer considered martyrs. Their graves, scattered throughout Chongqing, were left untended or built over in the years that followed.

—⟋⟋—

The Cultural Revolution passed to a new era. No one remembered my sister any more. The action that had cost her life became just another remote incident. I finally grew up and moved to the United States, where I can choose not to believe.

In the spring of 2002 I revisited my home city after fourteen years. I could no longer find my sister's grave. The Normal School had become the Normal University with a lot more buildings than I remembered. The stream was still there, but I was told that it had changed its path because of a big flood years before. The flood had also washed out the old wooden bridge. On the new concrete bridge, built after the flood, farmers were selling lunch to the university students. No one could tell me the original position of the old bridge. So I lost all clues to the location of my sister's grave.

In disappointment I turned to Sha'ping Park, less than a mile from the Normal University and the Third Middle School. There I found that the Red Guards' Martyrs Cemetery had been renamed the Cultural Revolution Graveyard. The way these Chinese words read, the name can be interpreted as either a graveyard that buried the Cultural Revolution or a graveyard that was built during the Cultural Revolution. This is the only Red Guard graveyard remaining in China.

Inside the high, ivy-covered stone walls, more than a hundred large granite tombstones stood like a gray forest, with weeds and wild trees encroaching. The engraved calligraphy of Chairman Mao's inscription "Long Live Martyrs" could still be seen on many of the weathered stones. There were wilted flower bouquets left on some tombs. I remembered that only a week ago was April 5 and the Qingming festival, a traditional time for mourning the dead.

I did not hold much hope for finding Ai Shu-Quan's grave, as many did not have names or the names could no longer be read. So it was consoling when I saw the engraved characters "Martyr Ai Shu-Quan" on the base of a tombstone. I had never met him, but I had heard his name from my sister. On August 3, 1967, Ruo-Dan had written in her journal:

This afternoon, just as I walked to the Red Building after my nap, I heard someone saying Ai Shu-Quan had died. I didn't believe it; I thought they were making a bad joke. But shortly after, 'Fishing Boat' returned with Ai Shu-Quan's body. Everyone was in extreme grief and indignation! They shot bullet after bullet to the sky. I couldn't believe my eyes: just the night before yesterday he was well, chatting with us about the current situation…

The next day she wrote:

Last night (I) did not go to bed until 2 a.m. This morning, learning that the Martyr's family had arrived, I hurriedly went to the troop's office. Sorrowful cries came out of the room before I reached it. They were from Martyr Ai Shu-Quan's mother, sister and father. It broke my heart. Ai Shu-Quan was a leader of our troop; he got along with everyone well; he was always smiling. He treated revolutionary work earnestly, seriously, actively and responsibly. He is missed by everyone. We are waiting for his brother to see him the last time before burying him.

August 6:

Ai Shu-Quan's elder brother arrived. He is a student of Tianjin University. He stood in silence before the Martyr's body for a long time, touched him, then took off his own picture button of Chairman Mao and the (Red Guard) armband and put them on his brother. At this point his father could no longer hold his tears and cried loudly and bitterly. To avoid breaking the old man's heart further, he turned around and shed tears behind his father. How could I stop my tears…

XUJUN EBERLEIN

There are more pages about Ai Shu-Quan's death in Ruo-Dan's journal. Enough for me to associate him with my sister. It was almost as if I had found my sister's grave. He and my sister were the only two students from Third Middle School who died during the Cultural Revolution. It was the school's luck that it did not see as many deaths as other schools; it was our two families' misfortune that these two deaths had occurred to us.

I did not see any flowers at Ai Shu-Quan's tomb. Was he forgotten by his family? It hurt to realize that I hadn't brought flowers for him either. The wind was still, the distant river running silent, but I knew that it could all change in an instant. For some time I stood in front of Ai Shu-Quan's tombstone and longed for my paper-cut patterns.

This is a collection of photographs of the daily experiences of Filipino American World War II veterans who have immigrated to the United States in the 1980s and 1990s. These elderly veterans came to seek a better life. They still have hope that one day the U.S. government will finally honor their military sacrifices by restoring the medical and pension benefits they were originally promised by President Roosevelt during World War II, but were later denied by the Rescission Act of 1945.

THE LAST BATTLE

THE LAST BATTLE

by Gary Reyes

GARY REYES

THE LAST BATTLE

GARY REYES

GARY REYES

EQUITY for all Filipino WW II Veterans

EQUITY NOW

GARY REYES

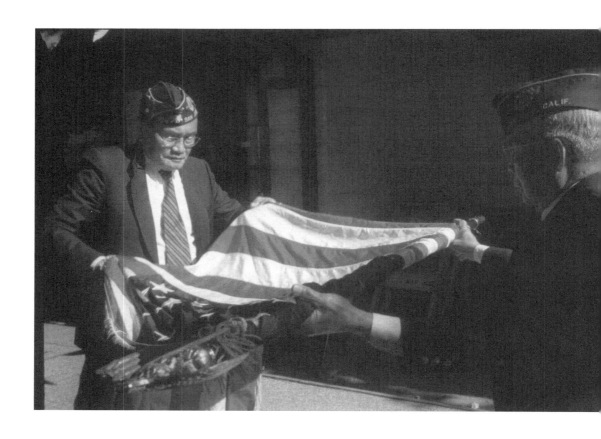

GARY REYES

GARY REYES

THE LAST BATTLE

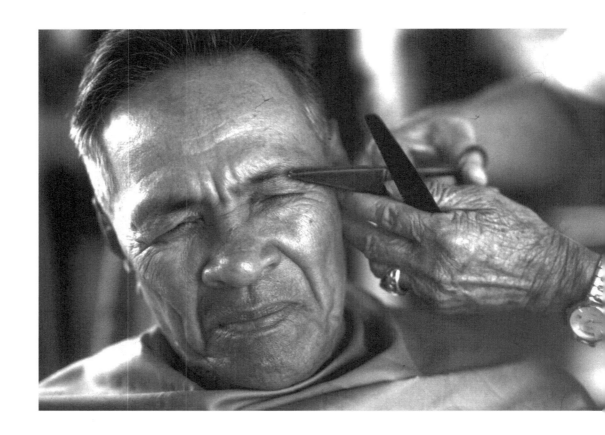

THE LAST BATTLE

GARY REYES

GARY REYES

THE LAST BATTLE

II. ABSENCE

MEMORIES

The author's paternal grandfather, José Francia, with his family in the
Philippines.

LIGHT AND SHADOW:
MEMORY OF A WAR, A WAR OF MEMORY

by Luis H. Francia

Against forgetting, the only death that really kills . . .
— Eduardo Galeano

How did it all start? With blood: spilling it; mixing it; generating it. With a young couple migrating from famine-stricken Ireland to the New World in the mid-nineteenth century. It begins — and it begins even before — with a young man from Spain seeking his fortune in his country's only Asian colony, a necklace of an archipelago strung out on a north-south axis. He had been preceded there three centuries before by Fernando Magallanes, a tough-as-nails Portuguese navigator working for the Spanish crown, who had stumbled on the islands in his expedition's epic voyage of circum-navigating the globe. He claimed the islands for Spain, for himself. Instead, the islands claimed him, his blood soaking a Visayan beach in ill-fated combat with the chieftain Lapu Lapu.

And so ensue tangled bloodlines, mixed-up histories, the global narrative of hybridity: part of my continuing story, one that includes *la fiesta y la iglesia* as well as Hollywood blondes, rock'n'roll, Converse sneakers, indomitable matriarchs, beliefs in animist spirits, and the formidable powers of psychics. Our middle-class family table included pig's blood stew, milkfish soup, *arroz à la Cubana*, *pan de sal*, hamburgers, and Coca-Cola. I might say, to willfully quote Rimbaud out of context, that my life was a feast where all wines flowed and all hearts were open.

The truth of the matter is, I hardly thought of my life or the lives of friends and family as a feast. I simply assumed that the variety of what we had, of what we were used to, was the natural state of things, this confluence of cultures: Filipino, Spanish, and American. For the writer that I became, such autobiographical elements with their troubling revelations, fascinating permutations, and deep-seated contradictions and historical roots took on the characteristics of a treasure trove, to be mined particularly once I began to understand the context, the history—with both a small and a large "h"—and the ways in which the society I grew up in had evolved. I am one hundred percent hybrid, mestizo, a mutt. And yet I can say with confidence that I am completely pure—not in the atavistic, narrow sense that has produced only tragedy in the last century, but in the sense of being unique, of being a point where several cultures intersect. I am beginning to understand what Roque Ferriols, a Jesuit and brilliant philosophy professor in university, tried to make us see: that we are all completely different and completely identical at the same time. Put another way: I am unique—just like everyone else.

—⁂—

Thinking of 1898 without thinking of 1899 is simply impossible. To me, they form a continuum, a war that had two phases: the first as the last year of Spanish dominion, pitting unlikely comrades-in-arms, Filipinos and Americans, against the Spaniards; the second, a bitter fight between erstwhile allies, and the beginning of American conquest. I associate these two phases with two faces, those of my grandfathers, *Lolo* Henry and *Lolo* Pepe. Because war is a predominantly masculine endeavor—women being far too smart for the rites of senseless bloodletting—it is Henry and Pepe I think of with regard to this war.

History distinguishes between the Spanish-American and the Philippine-American wars; in reality, it was one long war of greed against my forebears, who had in 1896 initi-  ated the first revolution against a Western power in Asia and subsequently declared independence in June of 1898. The enemy was the overriding desire of the West to cling to its nasty, addictive habits of imperialism; Spain had grown too old to keep it up, while America, virile, vigorous, brutish, was more than willing to take over the rapacious duties of dominance, indoctrination, and salvation—ironically, of a people who had this foolish notion that they were capable of redeeming themselves. Acting in the best Puritanical tradition, the Yankee felt it was necessary to destroy the country in order to save its residents.

Did Lolo Henry, captain in the U.S. Army, think of himself as a savior? No member of my family has any record of what he might have thought of the war and his role in it. In all likelihood he would have held—at the outset, anyway—with the stereotypical views of the *indios* whom President William McKinley determined needed to be "civilized and Christianized," conveniently ignoring the fact that Filipinos had their own vibrant culture and had, moreover, been Catholic for over three centuries. Many of the American officers had participated in the genocidal wars against Native Americans, of whom there was no thought of redeeming (whatever that might have meant), only of killing. And in the eyes of such men, like General "Howling Jake" Smith and Colonel Frederick Funston, Filipinos were no better than "Injuns."

Henry himself sought redemption of some sort. My maternal grandmother, Lola Agatona, provided that by injecting some color into his white soul and making him turn his back on repatriation once the war was over. What was there to return to? In the islands he found love, a comfortable way of living, immediate and privileged status that more than compensated for the absence of the familiar, if not the dear.

No letters to and from him exist, or none that I am aware of. He may have written to his brother James who lived on the West Coast, but not to his stepmother, a cruel woman whom he, according to my mother, detested. As a young man, even though he had thought of a medical career, he followed the tradition of seeking glory, fortune, and the definition of a masculine self achieved in combat by enlisting in the army. He served in Cuba first, before shipping out to Manila, by then a tattooed, seasoned fighter. My images of him have tended to be somewhat romantic. Not necessarily wrong, but incomplete (as they shall always be), predisposed by my mother's recollections of her dad, which continue to accrete as I spur her intermittently to do so. Affable, dashing, generous to kids, lover of animals, playful, etc. (My mother's views on her father are as positive as those on her mother are dark and unpleasant. Yet there is a lot of Agatona in her daughter.)

LUIS H. FRANCIA

On the other hand, Henry had no cause to be in the archipelago, except as a dutiful member of an illegitimate occupation force, that initially allied itself with the Philippine Revolution, and ended as the very enemy it had promised the Filipinos to defeat. For the War of Two Phases was also two-faced: the cover-up of imperial thievery with the smiley façade of enlightened benevolence. It is possible Henry might have shot and killed Filipino soldiers in battle. If he did, it was what was expected of him and what he was trained to do, but I can't help wonder what went through his mind.

As for José Francia, or Lolo Pepe, a member of the provincial landed gentry, he was older, and lived longer than Henry. The two never met, as Henry died in late middle age, when my mother was a fifteen year old. What would Lolo Pepe have thought of Lolo Henry? Of the War with Two Phases? He might have had ambivalent feelings about the 1896 Philippine Revolution, as his father José Sr. was a Creole, a half-blooded Spaniard and wealthy landowner in the green and fertile province of Laguna, not far from the port city of Manila. No doubt that wealth owed much to Luis, my great-great-grandfather, who used his privileged position as a Spanish émigré to his advantage. (And my question, that will forever remain unanswered: What sort of man was he?)

Pepe had no love for the *Amerikanos*. They were wannabes in the old game of empire. In the war against them, being a man of means he most likely helped the guerrillas on and around the holy mountain of Banahaw, where Magdalena, his hometown, sits at its foot. In the war's aftermath, fearing its contamination, Pepe apparently refused to speak English, though he could understand it. (This disdain didn't extend to the American automobile, for he was one of the first in Magdalena to own one.) I don't know if his views had changed by the time World War II erupted. By then, he was a few years away from death, and his eldest son, my father, had been married to my mother for four years, with my two older brothers already walking the dark tropical earth. By then too, the Americans had been in the archipelago more than forty years, and at war's end would be seen as liberators—a reversal in popular perceptions of them, in large part because of the deprivations and atrocities Filipinos suffered at the hands of the Japanese army.

The War of Two Phases has become over the years a fulcrum on which I turn the looking glass of memory on myself, my family, and the society I've always been a part of, and apart from. It has also helped shape—now more than ever, when Bush the Younger has waged a senseless, immoral war on Iraq, with rhetoric that recalls similar inflammatory language used in 1899—my relationship to America, a place constituted largely by outsiders, who perennially suspect other, more recent outsiders. The views that pop up on the screen of my imaginative memory differ markedly from those on official channels. The conventional narrative they construct avoids the personal. Mine is largely about the personal, for memory in this instance acquires the shape of a battlefield, a site to be contested, between imperial power and native resistance, between the thrust of a society relentless in its desire to forget and my own thirst for remembering. Who controls my memory controls me. Will it continue to be written by the victors, by Hollywood, with its seraglio of seductive images and infinitely mutable happy endings?

Unlike geographic territory, memory is never so neat. Its borders constantly shift, its guardians (whether an individual such as myself, or an institution) and its claims often contradictory, its voluminous files either in disarray, obscured, or brilliantly clear. Like an oracle, the truth in memory can set one free, free to move on. But there is memory and there is memory. I remember what I used to remember— memory of my memory—about the United States, which was partly the product of schooling, of the prevalence of American pop culture, and, in hindsight, the dim awareness of an Irish American grandfather, whose death before I or any of my siblings was born preserved a portrait of a kindly man: benevolent, tolerant, enlightened, democratic, and white. I invested the Americans I got to know with that portraiture, an act that conveniently masked their shortcomings, their all too human failings. They represented an America that was largely symbolic, a series of signs largely empty of substance. Now what I remember—both the jagged, haunting shards of American deceit, and the green fields of plenty and largesse—is frequently at odds with that. And perhaps it is in the gray shades of memory that I can locate the heart of the tension peculiar to being a Filipino American.

—◊—

LUIS H. FRANCIA

A few years ago, I was quite taken by *After Life,* a film by Hirokazu Kore Eda. In it, he fashions a beautiful and haunting meditation on memory, where the newly dead go through an orientation process—handled by a kind of bureaucracy in a halfway house—before proceeding on the trip to that country from which no traveler has ever returned. Each person selects a key memory to take along, and that memory is then re-created as a film and given to the person, so the journey can begin. Kore Eda contemplates the act of remembering, how it enables each one of us to have a context, a particular history, to ground us; how in fact memory becomes the very basis of *human* existence.

The analogous use and reference to cinema (for the film comments wryly on cinematic processes, and thus on itself as well) posits memory as a built-in visual archive, where the past can be viewed and re-viewed endlessly, constantly exercising tremendous power to shape the ways in which we view ourselves, whether as individuals or communal actors, and color the human landscapes we fashion. In its critique of memory, *After Life* implies complex, even contradictory, subtexts, one of which, it seems to me, is that memory, while springing from the past, subverts it, thus exposing it as a convenient fiction. If the past is always present and we the living are its bearers, can the past ever be the "past"? As Proust understood so brilliantly, to think of the past as time irretrievably lost is to misapprehend its nature: it exists, still, and all around us, whether as teacups and madeleines, or jottings in a diary, or a portrait above a mantel—it rears up, a horse in a corral longing to be set loose. (The last book in Proust's seven-volume novel, by the way, is titled *Time Regained.*) What has dropped from sight is the event itself, which flares up, blazes like a meteor across the sky, and vanishes. The imprint and/or recollection of the event is as light traveling in the aftermath of a stellar explosion: Light from dead stars continues to exist and unceasingly spreads. If, like astronomers, we have sensitive enough detectors, we can pick up these traces of light and decipher the stories they contain. And like celestial light, memories link being and non-being, the living with the dead.

That link was felt most keenly by the *manong,* young Filipino men, mostly from the working-class and peasantry, who came over in the early decades of the twentieth century to strike it rich and to send money to their families back home. In Bienvenido

Santos's poignant, heartbreaker of a story "The Day the Dancers Came," Fil, a homely middle-aged manong with no family of his own, except a roommate (Tony, a manong dying of cancer), hears of a troupe of Filipino dancers visiting Chicago, where he lives. He wishes to invite the graceful young men and women to a home-cooked meal so that "they would have something special to remember about us here when they return to our country. They would tell their folks: We met a kind old man...But what a cook that man was! And how kind!" Sadly, but not surprisingly, the dancers rebuff him. And Fil is left to confront the expatriate's eternal fear: to no longer count in the memories of those left behind. Living now in a country that seems not to have any recollection of him, he might as well be dead. And soon Tony, his only tangible link to home, will die. Someone else, even the unknown parents of the youngsters, must remember him, to keep him alive.

The poet Li-Young Lee writes, "Memory revises me." Indeed. But not only does it revise, memory creates me. Fanciful? Consider DNA, the molecular text which essentially writes the body. Built on memory, it incorporates lessons learned, or frailties still to be resolved, and passes these on from generation to generation. Embedded within me, this text irrefutably proves how, at a most fundamental level, memory determines my way of being in the world. It roots me literally to both sides of the Pacific. I am what I remember; I am what I am remembered as.

So while all that "bloody blundering business"—as one commentator described the Philippine-American War—transpired at a time when both of my grandfathers were young men and involved in the contest to shape or resist an empire, the war continues to impinge on and shape my consciousness—this essay being only one proof of this. I write not only about the memory of a war, but also about the war of and on memory, the struggle to replace a history I barely recognize with one I do, with one where I am an active soldier, willing to do a stint at the front lines, in the struggle to tear down the walls, and open up the gates.

It gets complicated, for the War of Two Phases contains many sides. Happy or unhappy, inevitably each one of us, each side, beholds the past but in a different fashion. This is why even if shared the past is so difficult to decipher, rendering conflicting versions a Rashomon-like exercise, and making colonialism's enduring impact reside, not solely in baroque churches or in such governmental forms as Congress, but, like a geological imprint, in the altered memory, the mutant psyche in Filipinos like me. Frantz Fanon knew intimately how demolishing a subject people's memory to replace it with that of the empire builders vastly facilitates colonial rule. In *The Wretched of the Earth*, he writes, "Colonialism is not satisfied merely with hiding a people in its grip and emptying the native's brain of all form and content. By a kind of perverted logic, it turns to the past of the oppressed people, and distorts, disfigures and destroys it."

The colonized interior—the past as neutered by the master's gaze—remains the hardest, and most forbidding, territory to reclaim from the invader. The journey looms as a perilous, Conradian voyage of darkness attended by a crew of impolitic doubts. Might not it be best to let sleeping dogs lie? What if the colonizers, murderous as they were, were right after all—that, before their arrival, we were inchoate sentences, all verbs and no subject? That we needed to be saved from ourselves? Memory looms as a prize commodity on the global marketplace: malleable, quantifiable, and above all profitable—memory as money. Tap into the aptly named memory banks and see the dollars flow!

Not surprisingly, the colonized view their subjugation the other way around, extracting the sorry facts from a white narrative, ever mindful of a time when America hijacked a young country's dreams and acts of self-determination. Such a voyage of recovery unfortunately is often awash in sentimentality. Many Filipino Americans tend to romanticize the place that their parents left behind, as counterweight to official history, which pushes them aside as bit players. As the late poet Alfrredo Navarro Salanga wrote:

> *The only problem is*
> *they don't think much*
> *about us*
> *in America.*

When America does remember us, it often does so in outmoded and insulting ways. Not long ago, I learned of the existence of the Military Order of the Carabao, founded in 1900 by American veterans of the War of Two Phases. Today, the secretive Order continues to thrive, its jingoistic spirit very much alive. Its membership includes top military brass, defense industry bigwigs, and officer/veterans of other American wars. Every year these overwhelmingly male bonders hold a gathering, known as the Wallow (a term more ironic than its members may suspect), where racist songs from the War of Two Phases are boisterously sung. The favorite marching ditty, "The Soldier's Song," offers up this chorus for the edification of all empire builders: "Damn, damn the insurrectos!/ Cross-eyed khakiac ladrones!/ Underneath the starry flag, civilize them with a Krag,/ And return us to our own beloved homes." "Insurrectos" replaced the original "Filipinos" as a cosmetic gesture of appeasement, though today, given Bush's playground view of the world as Us vs. Them, "insurrectos" has been supplanted by "terrorists," which can refer to any group or nation seen as a threat, real or imagined, to American security and global hegemony, and therefore a legitimate target for preemptive strikes, now part of official U.S policy. (The war on Iraq sprung out of a fevered, xenophobic, mistaken imagination, with no W.M.D.s or links to Al Qaeda found; with thousands of innocents killed, the war itself is unambiguously terroristic.) Clearly, the Order, and by extension the U.S. military, remembers the Philippine-American War as a kind of guilty, dirty secret—a memory that dare not speak its name. Nor is it surprising that the existence of such an atavistic body is not better known, for the Order fears light. When confronted, its apologists do a shuffle and cheerfully exclaim that it's all done in fun. (Yes, my dear fellows, but so was blackface.) In naming themselves after the ubiquitous beast of burden in Southeast Asia, the Order's ranks may reflect its simple-mindedness, its loyalty to the hand that feeds it, and its love for mud, but not that animal's love of light and openness. I think that perhaps the Order might rename itself after a more suitable life form, such as the cockroach, which thrives in dark, damp corners and feeds on detritus.

Immigrant parents, even as they encourage their offspring to assimilate seamlessly, betray their own homeward gaze. Having departed what in recollection glimmers like a distant utopia—because of dislocation, of racism in the new land—

they never fully arrive. Many are the clues, from the visible artifacts of the place left behind, ranging from cheerfully tacky giant wooden spoons and forks to more somber relics of crucifix and devotions to the Virgin Mary, to the infinite network of friends, relatives, and the complex, intricate, and irreplaceable system of personal narratives that bind all of them to a particular land—to "home." Children, as children will, mock these clues and yet mark them relentlessly, to investigate these paths that lead to nostalgia, revelation, desire, bitterness, and may just point the way to happiness. Their sense of their parents' prior lives often initiates a voyage of (re)discovery that could either be truly astonishing or depressingly trite.

Parents and offspring navigate continuously and simultaneously two, even three, rivers. It's a voyage Filipinos know pretty well: tricky, full of treacherous currents, twists, unexpected bends, sandbars, benign and dangerous creatures. Having survived depredations by the Spanish, the Japanese, and the Americans, we know a thing or two about uncertain voyages.

My own sense of the voyage is of a never-ending process. I see that voyage being revisited and tweaked, though they may not know it, when young Filipino Americans and urbanized Filipino youths appropriate hip-hop and rap, taking on the label of "blackness" simultaneously as a mantle of rebelliousness—for them, the heart of darkness has an entirely different meaning—and as a badge of pride meant especially to horrify (naturally) their elders. They may not know it, but their mimicry echoes the empathy Buffalo Soldiers, as African Americans in the army were known at the time of the war, showed the Filipino rebels, with whom they had more in common than with their white comrades-in-arms: the recognition the fraternity of the oppressed can bestow upon one another.

Their voyage can lead to a questioning of the rosy-hued views of the American presence in the islands that official narratives encourage. Let me start you out, dear reader, with just one fact and you can ferret out the rest: the deaths, mostly from starvation and disease, of at least 250,000 and possibly close to a million Filipinos (a seventh of the population then), most of them noncombatants. Massacres at places like Balanggiga and Bud Dajo foretell My Lai more than half a century later, revealing both the frustration and brutal character of the American campaign. The title of an essay by Mark Twain—who wrote impassionedly and brilliantly against America's imperialist designs on the Philippines—sums it up bluntly: "Thirty Thousand Killed a Million." Read it, and weep.

—⚹—

I cannot recall a specific moment when I learned about the Philippine-American War. There were no sudden bolts of lightning, no dramatic conversion on the way to Damascus. Certainly not at school, where history courses had a decidedly Eurocentric bent. Perhaps the implicit notion or fervent wish was that the Philippine nation-state had somehow sprung fully formed from the head of some deity into the modern age. The war and I approached each other through a process set in motion by two landmark events: the American war on Vietnam, and the imposition of martial law on the Philippines by Ferdinand Marcos in 1972. Living in New York at the beginning of the '70s, it was not difficult at all to see the huge gap between what the U.S. government was saying about the need for American intervention in Southeast Asia and the more persuasive realities of nationwide antiwar protests, body bags, racism, Cold War strategic positioning, etc.—all of which spoke eloquently to the divide, between the dark, voracious side of empire, and the utopian aspirations that America incorporated into its Constitution and formal ethos. Its adventurism in the Philippines had given the U.S. time to rehearse its "good cop/bad cop" roles in an ongoing schizophrenic, Jekyll and Hyde drama that's still being played out, most clearly today, in Iraq.

Marcos's tyrannical rule initiated a dirty war similar to dirty wars in Chile and Argentina, among other despotic regimes supported by the U.S. If the dark side of empire had not heretofore been evident to Filipinos, then Yankee support of a dictator should have revealed it all too clearly. For all his nationalist talk, Marcos was Washington's brilliant foster child, its best bet for keeping U.S. bases in the country, never mind that human rights violations under his regime were both deliberate and widespread. Washington's canard about preserving democracy was brazenly exemplified in 1981, when Vice President George Bush, on a visit to Manila, infamously toasted the Marcoses' "adherence to democratic principles." Marcos lasted until four glorious days in February of 1986, when the amazingly peaceful People Power uprising drove him and his loony, shoe-loving wife Imelda into exile. Watching TV—with its transfixing images of roses and rosaries, poems and personal courage facing down the regime's tanks and heavily armed soldiers, and being glued, in those pre-Internet days, to the radio—I was euphoric, as were most of my friends, Filipino and non-Filipino. Fed-up ordinary citizens had kicked a dictator's butt. Those incandescent days tied us in 1986, if only briefly, to our forebears in 1896 taking up arms against the Spanish.

At the outset of martial law, I helped found an anti-Marcos monthly *Ningas Cogon*, or *Brush Fire*, which despite minimal funds, lasted for almost a decade and proved to be a thorn in the side of the New York-based Philippine Consulate. (*Ningas* began in Manila as *Imelda's Monthly*, a pre-martial law satirical broadsheet, one of whose founders was named Imelda. With the imposition of martial law, and Imelda—the shoe-lover, not the founder—on the warpath, *Imelda's Monthly* had to fold, only to resurface in New York as *Ningas Cogon.*) The monthly's members were blacklisted; fortunately the government minders misspelled my name as Franco Luis—an appellation I promptly affixed to my pieces.

My opposition to the war on Vietnam grew in proportion to my disgust with U.S. support for the Marcos regime. I started to do research on the War of Two Phases and wrote two short essays on it for *Ningas*. It was at this time, too, that I discovered Twain's caustic essays, penned on behalf of the Boston-based Anti-Imperialist League, on American intervention in a Southeast Asian country that had just established itself as an independent nation. Anti-Vietnam War activists had resurrected this little-known aspect of a quintessentially American writer (for a while his daughter, his literary executor, excluded his lion-hearted, anti-imperialist writings from posthumous collections as these didn't quite fit his folksy image) so that the 1899 war, so distant before, suddenly became up close and personal. The war on Vietnam turned out to be an old one after all, just with high-tech weapons and electronic media there to convey disturbing images. Had TV existed in 1899, I am convinced the war against the Philippines would have ended as the war against Vietnam did.

The Philippine-American War did provide the occasion for some of the earliest (if not the earliest) American propaganda films: Thomas Alva Edison's short reels of the Spanish-American War (which elided the war on the Philippines) purported to be the real thing, when in fact the most dramatic were staged and shot in then bucolic New Jersey, with crude, made-up scenarios constructed along racial and ideological beliefs. Blacks play the insurrectos, and are easily defeated, reluctant warriors ready to flee at the first sign of combat, ready presumably to submit to the uplifting values of strict but wise white taskmasters. These are the reels that clue us in on what America, more than a hundred years after, chooses to take along on its voyage. The only lesson it seems to have learned from the Philippine-American War—and from such other wars as that on Vietnam—has not been in humility or soul-searching but in figuring out ever-more efficient battlefield strategies. The distance from hamletting to shock and awe has proved to be a short one after all.

Light travels. Images resonate. The war goes on.

And on. Once again, U.S. soldiers loom large in the archipelago—still desirous of civilizing us, this time not with a Krag, but with M-16s and Apache helicopters—even though the Philippine Constitution forbids the presence of foreign troops on native soil and in 1991 the Philippine Senate (in a rare act of independent thinking so sorely missed in the country's post-World War II leadership) terminated the treaty under which U.S. bases had operated in the country for close to a century. Once again, Washington promises to aid Manila in fighting a common enemy, trotting out shopworn rhetoric, although what that common enemy may be is left unclear. Once again, it prattles on about democracy and freedom, about "special relations"—the phrase favored by the United States whenever its interests are the topic under discussion, and meant to recall imagined times when colonizers and their "little brown brothers" fraternized happily and willingly. Once again, the U.S. "remembers" but in ways that threaten an archipelagic state with even more fragmentation: re-membering as an act of dis-membering. Once again, I watch a disturbingly familiar film following an old, well-rehearsed script. Déjà vu? D'Asia vu.

Memory mutates, the U.S. metamorphoses from unbidden ally to betrayer and foe to occupier and colonizer, then to friend and generous godfather. This time, it no longer is the Philippine-American War, but the nebulous, globe-girdling, seemingly endless "War on Terrorism," in which the country has been labeled "the second front"—a designation that the Philippine government, puzzlingly enough, seems pleased to accept, even though the country has no foreign enemies. The ostensible target is the Abu Sayyaf, a violently dangerous but small, essentially criminal, gang, whose ideology, if it can be called that, is mainly to make money through kidnappings. The country does have two long-standing insurgencies, one regional and Muslim (the Moro Islamic Liberation Front, or M.I.L.F.), and one country-wide and Maoist (the New People's Army, or N.P.A.). Manila has been engaged intermittently in peace talks with both, but talks with the latter are effectively dead in the water, due to the U.S. classifying the N.P.A. as "terrorist"—the one-label-fits-all approach a legacy of 9/11.

The rubble of the twin towers buried more than their unlucky victims, entombing as well on the national level any coherent, rational analysis and policy that isn't driven by the twin engines of primal fear and a cynical, evangelical, extreme right-wing agenda. And it has resurrected—out of the seemingly placid, albeit artificial, lake of diversity—vicious racism, a fear and loathing of the dark-skinned other—the *Creature from the Black Lagoon* redux. Examples abound of palpable nostalgia for a supposedly simpler time, when people of color knew their place. Personally, what I see is difference, *my* difference, being held against me, my sense of self and place undermined, my legitimacy as a civic being called into question in a war that can be as murderous as that of bullets and bombs—and certainly more deceptive.

That same subtext (difference as anathema) is playing out in Muslim southern Mindanao (and of course in the Middle East) which bears the brunt of hostility stemming in large part from the Orientalist manner in which Moros (the term for Filipino Muslims) have always been remembered by the Christian government to the north and by an American military that fought there once before. Filipinos, Muslim and non-Muslim alike, still discern the light-traces from earlier fallouts, like the infamous massacre at the aforementioned Bud Dajo. In 1906 U.S. soldiers, under the command of General Leonard Wood, slaughtered 900 mostly unarmed Muslim men, women, and children. Why should this latest round of search-and-destroy be any different? Why should we wonder when Moros resent having to see themselves as, to use Czeslaw Milosz's words, "a nation of the excluded, whose day begins and ends with the awareness of failure"? Nor should we be surprised when many of them believe the War of Two Phases, as far as their homeland is concerned, has never really ended. And for those mostly Christian Filipinos who blithely welcome the reinsertion of American troops, their short or even nonexistent memories parody unknowingly the initial goodwill of that fin de siecle generation who, knowing little about the bluecoats, had at least the very good excuse of naïveté.

—⁊⁊—

Light travels. Images resonate, are turned upside down. Bandits are revealed as heroes, and heroes as outlaws. Acts of bravery or acts of treachery? Liberation or enslavement? Was that a war or just an extraordinarily intense relationship working its way towards mutual resolution and accommodation? Fraternity, perhaps? Yes, but surely of the Cain and Abel type, sans *liberté*, sans *egalité*.

In the interaction of light and shadow, in a film that keeps playing in my mind—and I will insist to the keepers of the afterlife that I need to bring more than one—my grandfathers Henry and Pepe keep appearing, moving confidently through corridors and opening doors onto surprising vistas. They seem to be on the verge of saying something. I wish to feel the tug of connection strongly, to hear them speak, issue directives, claim me as their grandson. And I wait impatiently, eager to listen, to learn from their experience of war.

They fill the screen repeatedly, putative brothers and fathers-in-law, sometimes in clear focus, sometimes in closeup, sometimes as fuzzy images, and sometimes just as a felt presence—the sort you get when you enter a room and know someone has just left. Pepe and Henry are stars in a larger drama that I have an expanding sense of and that continues to play out.

What lines will they, will memory, speak? What other scenes will unfold? I have a sense of its beginning, but how will this film end? How do I edit it? And where do I cut?

The author, far right, with his parents and brother, shortly after arrival in Malaysia. The photos were taken by the United States High Commissioner for Refugees (U.N.H.C.R.).

CROSSING THE SOUTH CHINA SEA

by John Vu

In 1979 my parents, younger brother and I fled Vietnam by boat across the South China Sea. I was seven years old, my brother five. Throughout the years, no matter how I tried to suppress the experience of drifting out at sea for three days and four nights, I couldn't do it, partly because that experience had seared itself indelibly in my heart and mind, partly because my parents would always bring it up.

Ba, my father, and Ma, my mother, brought up stories of Vietnam and the war and its aftermath because they wanted us never to forget, and to remember our history so that we, their only reason for escaping Vietnam, could form a future free from that painful past. This is my attempt to remember our history and the history of countless other refugees who took to the seas after the fall of Saigon in 1975.

I chose to structure this episode as a "short story" because I felt I could best evoke the immediacy and emotion of our experience — still so palpable to me — of what I witnessed, thought and felt. Though I remember the essence of conversations around me on the boat, I couldn't have recalled the passages of dialogue without the help of my parents. I dedicate this story to them.

"Get up, son. Hurry, we have no time to lose."

"Ba, why? What's going on?"

Ba was in a panic, and proceeded to wake up Ma and younger brother Quoc.

"Hurry, get dressed. We must leave right away!"

Ba's voice grew louder and more desperate. I looked at the clock on our wall and turned to the window. It was five in the morning and dark out. Then I looked over at Ma, who was already up trying to wake Quoc from his sleep.

"Son, get up, get up, we have to leave."

"Ma, what's happening? Where are we going?" I asked. Ma put her hand on my cheek as she usually did when she wanted to comfort me, "Don't worry, son. Everything's fine. Don't ask any questions."

"You have everything?" Ba asked as Ma retrieved a suitcase of valuables from the closet. The night before, Ma had packed a suitcase full of her favorite belongings —traditional *áo dàis*, silk scarves, and a couple pairs of shoes. I had no idea why Ma had packed her things, and when I'd inquired, she merely told me that it wasn't anything, that I shouldn't ask so many questions.

"Put this sweater on, it's cold outside," Ma implored, pulling the sweater over my head.

"Ma, where're we going?"

"Don't question your mother, Vuong!" Ba's tone now serious, "Do what she says."

The next thing I knew, Ma had layered several sweaters on Quoc and me, one over another, until she couldn't get anymore on. I felt hot and uncomfortable, but remained quiet.

Ma pulled a precious wooden box full of gold, diamonds and jade from under the bed. Ba and Ma had smuggled what valuables they could from our jewelry business in Saigon before the Viet Cong confiscated it. Intently, I watched her hide the jade bracelets, gold rings, and diamond earrings down her blouse and into her pants.

A few minutes passed before we were out the door and into the darkness.

The persistent thought running through my mind was that something was wrong, and that perhaps we were leaving our home for good. I turned to Ba and asked him where we were going, to which he only said, "We're going to a better place son, a place where we will be free of the Viet Cong."

I was too young to know much about the Viet Cong, only that they were our enemies. After the Viet Cong rolled into Saigon with their tanks, they occupied our home and jewelry business. Soldiers guarded our house and frisked me every time I went out to play. After stopping and searching me, they'd ask me questions like, "Where're you going? Who're you going to play with? What are their names?" The Viet Cong were suspicious of everything and everyone. There was always a guard keeping watch over us to make certain that we weren't smuggling any of our valuables out of the house. That's what Ba meant by being free of the Viet Cong.

The road to Kien Giang Province was dark. Ba led us with a small flashlight, first through the woods, then through a valley and across rice meadows. We couldn't see anything save the dirt path at our feet; now and then a pocket of fireflies danced in the air, creating a soft, subtle light. I was transfixed by their glowing beauty, how they died and came alive, again and again. Crickets and other nocturnal insects were alive with song.

For a long while, we walked in the dark, weaving our way through jungle and dirt trails. When we got to the fishing inlet at Tac Cau, I noticed a swarm of bodies swaying back and forth. There were hundreds of people hovering around the small port, pushing and shoving each other to board. The arguing and hollering echoed through the air as agitated flashlights pierced holes in the darkness.

"Stay together," Ba ordered, "hold on to my hand and don't let go." Ma had a tight grip of my left hand while Ba led us with my right. We were strung together hand to hand like the jade rocks in Ma's necklace.

"Look for boat number eighty. We need to get on that boat, boat number eighty," Ba said over and over.

"How will we find it?" Ma asked. "It's too dark. There're too many people."

"Don't worry, just don't let go of the kids."

As we made our way to the dock, people were jostling for position, fighting to

113

get aboard boat number eighty with all their bags and suitcases. Ba fought through the swaying crowd, parting our way to the front. When we got to the edge of the dock, a big, strong man was pushing people back, trying to prevent some from sneaking on deck. Another man called out the last names of those who had bought permission to board. When our name was called, Ba elbowed our way to the front, at which point the man acknowledged Ba and let us through. As we stepped onto the wooden plank, the man in charge told Ma that there wasn't any room for her suitcase, then grabbed the suitcase from her and tossed it overboard. "What'd you just do!" Ma erupted. "You told us we were allowed to bring one suitcase. All of my valuables are in there, the only things I own!" Ba stepped in and restrained Ma from plunging into the ocean after it.

As we climbed on the deck, one of the captain's assistants, a dark wiry fisherman, directed us to the back of the boat, while the family behind us was sent down the hold. In the next few minutes, the deck was flooded with people. Ba positioned us against the side of the boat, away from the engine. People jammed in from all sides. Someone jabbed me in the side with an elbow. Another pushed me from the back. Ba and Ma shielded Quoc and me with their arms, protecting us from the enclosing crowd. Arguments broke out among people around us as they shoved each other for a seat on the wooden deck.

"This is my space! I'm saving it for my sister," one woman shouted.

"Your sister's not here," one of the assistants replied, "So move over."

The woman wailed uncontrollably, "Phuong! Sister Phuong! Where are you, Phuong! Phuong! Phuong!" People pushed and fought for space.

After our boat was crammed past capacity, the engine sputtered, spewing out black smoke. Slowly, we drifted out of port. Staring at the bay moving away from us, I felt a pang well up in my chest. For a long time, I sat motionless watching the waves lap the shore.

"Ma, where're we going?"

Ma paused for several seconds. "We're leaving the country, son," Ma said. "We're leaving Vietnam, son."

Ba put his arm around Ma's shoulders and gave her an embrace, which I had never seen him do before. "Don't cry, dear. We're doing it for the children. We have to do it for the children." I'd never seen Ma distraught like this before. I nestled myself beneath her arms and wiped the tears now trickling down her cheeks. "Ma, why are you crying?" She enclosed her arms around my neck, put her damp cheek against mine, closed her eyes, and inhaled the scent of my skin.

In silence, people stared back at the shore. Others covered their faces with their hands.

"We're really leaving our country," a woman next to us said ruefully.

"Shhh...everything will be fine," the man next to her responded as he caressed the woman's hand and wiped the tears streaming from her eyes.

At that moment, a pressing heaviness descended upon my chest as I tried to make sense of what was happening. Then it hit me that we would probably never return, that I would never again see my friends at school, that I would no longer be able to swim in the creek down the road, that I would no longer be able to climb trees to pick carambola and mangosteen, nor catch and raise baby sparrows.

Minutes after leaving Tac Cau bay, the engine of our boat choked to a stop, sending black fumes into the air. Again, the commotion began.

"What's wrong? What's wrong?"

"Why are we slowing down?"

"What's happening?"

"The engine stopped."

"Why now!"

"Mother of Jesus, please help us," Ma muttered, her hands clasped in prayer, her body rocking back and forth. In confusion, people shifted and looked to each other for answers, their eyes darting from left to right.

"We can't go back," one man said.

"They'll catch and imprison us," another added.

"The Viet Cong will kill me!"

"I'd rather drown than be captured by them."

"Heavens, please save us."

"Stay calm, stay calm," the captain tried to assure us. "We'll fix the engine, please stay calm."

Our flimsy five-by-seventeen-meter vessel was only built for a few fishermen. The weight of the boat was more than the engine could handle. The captain initially informed Ba that there would be 150 people on board. By the time we pushed away from shore, our boat was holding nearly 300 escapees.

For the next several hours, we tried to stay calm as the captain and his mechanics worked on the engine. After the engine bellowed a few times, it finally started. The sighs of relief ignited simultaneously.

"Thank heavens," Ma praised, her arms outstretched towards the sky. Ba closed his eyes and gave a sigh so deep I thought he was going to faint. Then without hesitation, we charged full throttle towards the vast open sea.

III

As we drifted toward international waters, the tide picked up and the ripples turned into waves. The wind began to howl. The rocking of our boat, which was slight at Tac Cau bay, intensified a few miles into the South China Sea, becoming increasingly violent the further we drifted from shore. With each wave, our boat dipped and rose, reared and tossed from side to side. Walls of water grew on each side as we plunged into deep troughs of darkness. Then, with as much thrust, the waves pushed us to their foaming crests as we collectively gasped. I wrapped my arms around Ba's body, locked my fingers together, and held on tight. With each crashing wave, the thought of death out at sea became more and more palpable to me, the constant image of being swallowed up. I imagined my hands struggling to stay afloat, then slowly sinking into the ocean.

The sea thrashed our vessel for what seemed like an eternity. In one moment, the stern of the boat shot skyward and in the next it plunged seaward, jolting us forward, then pulling us backward. The hits were unpredictable; just when I was prepared to be propelled forwards, I was shot backwards, then sideways, sideways and backwards. People wailed in panic. Some yelled to the sky while others closed their eyes in resignation. With all my strength, I held onto Ba's body to prevent myself from being thrown against the others, who, also in desperation, grabbed whatever and whomever they could to weigh themselves down. For some fifteen minutes, the sea rocked our boat. Then suddenly, the winds calmed and the waves subsided. Our vessel resumed its slow bobbing, as before we hit the storm. The screaming now gave way to a chilling calmness as we tried to understand the feeling of fear and relief that had overtaken us in such a short period of time.

"We're alive," Ma sighed heavily. "We're alive."

As soon as the waves relented, the seasickness started. Moans of discomfort began coming from the belly of the boat.

"I need air, please, I can't breathe," the voice of a woman made its way from the hold. Then other voices.

"I can't breathe."

"We need air."

"Let us out."

"People are fainting down here."

"There's no room up here," one of the captain's assistants replied. "I'm sorry but you're going to have to hang in there."

Other moans ensued. More people began complaining that they too needed air. Then angry voices protesting, demanding that they be given air.

"If we can't go on deck, then we'll cut out a hole down here," one man said. "We need air. People are fainting."

"No! You can't do that!" another yelled. "We'd all sink."

"The boat will fall apart," Ba added. "There's too much weight. It'll break apart."

I thought about the possibility that at any moment our boat could fall apart from soaking up too much water, like my paper boats falling apart in our backyard pond. The captain and those on deck pleaded with the passengers in the hold to hang on, that soon we'd be rescued or land ashore. After some discussion, the captain and his crew were able to persuade the passengers in the hold that it was foolish to carve a hole in the upper part of the hull, and that those in poor condition would be able to come on deck for fresh air. The few who fainted were brought to deck and resuscitated. Then one by one, those who were short of breath were allowed up for fresh air. It occurred to us how lucky we were to be on deck.

Slowly, the hours passed. We searched for lights in the dark, hoping to be rescued by an international ship. It was known that "mercy ships" from other countries rescued refugees out at sea. Our hope hung on being saved by an international ship.

To notify any nearby ships of our presence, the captain and his men lit a fire in one of our four metal water barrels, which was now empty. For half an hour or so, the clothes doused in gasoline burned, then went out. We waited another half an hour, and then burned more. In half-hour segments, we burned and waited, praying that someone would spot us. No one came.

Darkness gave way to an expectant day as we began to emerge from twilight. Slowly, the horizon came into view. The sky was intensely blue, cloudless, the kind that comes after the monsoon rains. In every direction, the world looked the same. Blue on blue, endless skies above a boundless ocean. The infinite expanse of the sea and sky made us feel finite and powerless.

The warmth of the rising sun thawed our limbs. As the day progressed, the air became hot, sticky and stifling. At its zenith, the sun was scorching. We held our jackets and shirts over our heads to shield ourselves from the rays. The heat and humidity brought with it overpowering odors of sweat and vomit, wood and rotten fish that rose from the hold. Down below, there was no place to use the bathroom, so some went where they were. For those more embarrassed, buckets were passed down and around, and every now and then, passed back up and emptied overboard. Each time a bucket was passed up from the hold, the vomit, urine, and feces emanated a stench so unbearable that I gasped, plugging my nose to prevent myself from vomiting.

Undulating on the ocean, we were given meager rations of water and small portions of rice porridge, dried shrimp and fish sauce. It wasn't enough. My stomach howled constantly; every slurp of rice porridge made me yearn for more. Slowly I relished a small cup of the best porridge I'd ever had. Ba and Ma gave Quoc and me their portions.

After the meal, I managed to weave my way through the crowd to the overhanging potty at the back of the boat. Squatting over the hole cut out between my feet I was captivated by the beauty of the current with its dazzling emerald and white crests. As I gazed at the water flowing behind the rudder, I imagined what life was going to be like without my friends, without our house, without the fields in which I spent my time. I already missed our tree house and the hills and meadows where in the afternoons we caught butterflies and praying mantises. As I watched the current flow, I thought about our dog Mimi and how we left her behind with a neighbor; I thought about my red fighting cricket; I thought about the hens and ducks in the yard. A tear fell from my cheek into the ocean.

IV

The second night was clear, cold and penetrating. We were in complete darkness save for the stars trembling in the crisp, bluish sky. I'd never seen so many before. Quoc and I passed the time counting the stars, first the bright ones, then the dim ones. When we lost track, we began counting the spaces in between.

I was now glad that Ma had made us wear layers of clothing. A few flashlights and candles periodically lit holes in the air, revealing the haggard faces of people huddled together for warmth. Every now and then, a large wave crashed against the side of the boat. With each hit, I ducked beneath Ba's arms to shield myself from the sheets of icy water raining down on us. The salt grains in my hair and on my face made me itch all over.

The captain ordered his men to burn more rags. This time, instead of burning rags in half-hour segments, they burned them in hour segments because there was a limited supply of gasoline, and there was no telling how many days or weeks we would drift at sea. Though our hopes hung on being rescued by a "mercy ship," we realized that it might not happen. We burned rags, then waited, burned more rags, then waited.

To contain our fears and worries, which intensified each time a wave thrashed against the side of the boat, people took to intervals of song and storytelling. Solemnly, an old man began playing his bamboo flute. Ba hummed along to the tune. Some sang traditional Vietnamese hymns of love and loss, while others dreamt and told stories about faraway places and people they'd seen at the cinema or heard about from relatives and friends.

"In America, everyone's well off," one man said.

"How do you know?" another asked.

"That's what my brother says. He lives there."

"Yes, and everyone has a car," another added.

"They say in France, there's freedom," the woman next to us chimed in. "That's where I want to go."

"Ma, I want to go home," Quoc whined, "I want to go home."

"Don't cry son, everything's going to be all right." Ma put her nose against Quoc's face and inhaled deeply as she rocked him in her lap.

As the hours passed, some people began to talk about whether we would ever make it. The more rags we burned, the less hope we had of being saved. The captain and his assistants told stories of their adventures out at sea to try to assuage the doubts that arose as the hours persisted, with no sign of a rescue ship.

"Where are we?" Ba asked one of the assistants.

"I don't know."

"How much longer until we reach land?"

"According to the captain, we should arrive soon."

"How soon?"

"Soon."

"Where're we headed?" Ma asked.

"Somewhere."

"Where?"

"Does it matter?"

The assistant was right. It really didn't matter where we were going. The only thing that occupied our minds was being rescued or reaching land.

I was now accustomed to the motion of the sea. The constant rocking back and forth, the lapping of the water against the boat, the dipping and rising of the horizon: these things became a part of our existence. Unable to lie down, our bodies began to ache. Quoc complained about not being able to stretch his legs. Ma lost sensation in her thighs from holding us in her lap. Ba periodically complained about the sharp shooting pains in his back. Like everyone else, I was exhausted, worn out from hunger, thirst and lack of sleep, and from sitting in the same position for long stretches at a time. Knots formed in my lower back and shoulders, which twitched in spasms every now and then. It was difficult to shift positions without feeling the aches and pains that had become a part of my body. There were too many people and no room to stretch. Hemmed in between bodies, Ba had Quoc and me on his lap, one on each knee, for hours at a time, until his legs went numb; then Ma took her turn cradling us.

Out in the dark, shots rang out.

A collective scream reverberated through the air. Everyone shuffled in panic.

"Mother of Jesus!" Ba gasped.

"What's happening? What's happening?" Ma asked.

"We're being hit by pirates," Ba's lips quivered. "Thai pirates. Stay calm, stay calm."

The shots rang out again. Boom! Boom! The pirates had seen our fire.

"Heavens, please help us, please help us," Ma heaved. Ma put her arms around my shoulders as Ba clung to Quoc, who was now crying. Nestled within Ma's arms, I shook nonstop.

Suddenly our vessel wobbled as the pirates careened their boat into ours. The shrieks broke out again, this time louder than before. They flashed us with a large light, and then fired another shot.

"Listen up! Listen up!" a skinny teenager yelled in Vietnamese through a hand speaker.

"Do as we say or you will die!" he hollered as his partners waved knives and pointed guns at us.

After swinging their rope over and locking our bows together, the pirates forcefully shuttled some people across to their boat in order to clear room to begin their inspection.

"You, you and you, come now!" one of them demanded, while his collaborators pointed their guns directly in the faces of people seated at the stern. He was

121

JOHN VU

Vietnamese, like the teenager. After clearing some room on our deck, a few more men came across toting guns, shouting and demanding, in broken Vietnamese, that we hand over valuables. "Hand over jewelry now!" They kept yelling as they slithered their way through the crowd collecting whatever jewelry they could. There was some initial resistance, which quickly gave way to compliance after one of the women was smacked across the face with the butt of a gun for refusing to give up her jade bracelet.

As one of the raiders made his way to the back of the boat, Ma clutched me. Then Ma scraped the side of the boat with her fingers and rubbed her forehead and face with the dirt she had gathered. I noticed other women and girls doing the same thing, rubbing grime on their faces. "Give me your valuables now!" The teenager shouted at Ma. Ba panicked and told Ma to give him everything she had. Trembling, Ma took off her jade necklace, earrings, and wedding ring and handed them over to the teenager. Then suddenly, I felt one of his cold, calloused hands down my shirt, searching to see if I was wearing a necklace. My body contracted in shock as I gave out a cry, pulling away fearfully.

"Please don't hurt my son," Ma pleaded. "He has nothing."

The teenager paused and looked at me for an instant, and for an instant, I looked into his deep black eyes; then he moved on to someone else.

Minutes trickled by. The pirates took their time. They searched everyone and took anything of any value and assaulted people when they had to—earrings were torn from earlobes, rings yanked from fingers, bracelets snatched.

As the pirates were retreating to their boat after the raid, they blasted several rounds into the darkness. As they fired, they tore a young girl away from her parents. Then they took another girl.

"Don't anyone move! Don't fucking move!" one of them ordered as his accomplice grabbed and lifted a young teenage girl across the bow and into their boat.

The girl's father lunged after the attacker, but was immediately clubbed down by the butt of a gun.

"Don't fucking do anything stupid!" the assailant yelled.

"Loan, Loan, my baby, please don't take my baby!" the girl's mother pleaded, her body restrained by another attacker.

The girl kicked, screamed and tried to free herself, but her captor was too strong.

"Please don't take my girl, Loan, my daughter!"

"You devils, return my daughter," the girl's father demanded, his face bloody from the blow. Two pirates restrained him.

Then another young girl was torn from the arms of her parents.

"Stop them, stop them! Don't take my daughter, please don't take my daughter!"

The girl's parents tried to throw their bodies at the kidnappers but were restrained by other frightened refugees.

"Please, sister. There's nothing we can do. They'll kill us all," one of the crewmembers said as he held the girl's mother back while another restrained the girl's father. From Ma's arms, I trembled. Beads of cold sweat poured down my forehead. The shouting and the girls' helpless cries stabbed my eardrums. The beating of my heart grew louder and louder until I couldn't hear the screaming anymore. I looked at Ma's face to help me understand the tightness welling up in my chest and the blood rushing to my head. But her weeping gestures only deepened the terror that I felt. I looked at Ba. With his arms wrapped around Quoc, Ba sat motionless.

As the wailing and shouting grew, the pirates unleashed several additional rounds of gunfire, temporarily silencing the weeping. Then the pirates retreated cautiously with their guns and knives pointed at us and vanished back into the dark.

V

On the third morning out at sea, someone yelled, "Land, land, I see land!"

"Where? I don't see anything," Ma said.

"Over there, there, you see it?" Ba replied.

I saw a thin black line, thinner than a strand of hair, sketched on the horizon.

"It's the Philippines. That must be the Philippines," someone said.

"No, it can't be," Ba said, "We haven't gone that far."

Squeezing his hand, Ma turned to Ba and smiled with a happiness I'd never seen before. Tears sparkled in her eyes. Quoc, not knowing what was happening, asked, "Are we home Ma? Are we home?"

"Yes, son, we'll be home soon."

As the conversations regarding where we were headed were thrown around, the captain got up and informed everyone that we were headed toward Malaysia. What part of the country and on which island he didn't know. In fact, it really didn't matter where or what country we were headed towards, so long as we got there. Slowly, beautifully, the land grew out of the sea, moving toward us.

As we neared the port, several coast patrollers intercepted us. Five boats drew near our vessel.

We didn't have permission to enter port, one of the Malaysian patrollers told us as he signaled with his gun for us to turn around.

"We have no place to go, we've been robbed by pirates, we have no more food and water," the captain explained. "People are dying on this boat. Please let us in!"

The port authorities again told us we didn't have permission to enter, and that we had to land somewhere else.

"Please, we'll die if you don't let us in," one man said.

"Why don't you kill us right now then!" another added.

A couple of the men on our boat threatened to jump overboard and swim to shore if we weren't allowed in. Ma, along with the others, got on her knees and pleaded for sympathy, but their cries went unheeded. The Malaysians said they were under strict orders to bar us from entering. After several minutes, the Malaysians formed a blockade with their patrol boats, and threatened to pull us out themselves if we didn't comply with their orders.

"We can't go back now!" Ba yelled to the captain, "We can't go back!"

Blockaded by the Malaysian patrol boats, we had no other choice but to find a different place to land. Slowly, we circled around and headed back out to sea.

On the way out of the port, people yelled and cursed the captain for turning around. Some tried to enter the cabin to take the helm, but the assistants blocked them from doing so. To allay our fears, the captain promised that we would try to dock when it got dark, even if that meant having to confront the Malaysians. We swung around to the other side of the port and waited. Once it got dark, we charged the island with as much speed as we could. Several hundred yards from land, the captain shut off the engine. Silently, we coasted for several interminable minutes, then crashed thirty yards from shore.

A painting by the author of her father's childhood home.

WAR DWELLINGS

by Anooradha Iyer Siddiqi

I am designing a Center for Meditation as a joint project with my father. He owns a piece of land in West Virginia that he has always intended to develop. It is a wooded, steep site, with a stream running through it. He once asked me to draw up architectural plans for residential apartments on the property. I tried to get excited about the opportunity to realize my own design, but we stumbled over the problems of construction on the property. The soil was unpredictable, the grade too dramatic to maximize its real estate value. The project went on hold. We talked about the possibility of building one freestanding house on the reliable portion of the land, but at a time that he was contemplating retirement, my dad didn't want to think about building a new home. The project stayed on hold, and I began to think he should just sell the property. Five days after he retired, my father was diagnosed with an advanced stage of lung cancer. He immediately began preparing for battle, allied with medication and with a personal goal. He wanted to build. The right project for this land became clear to him. He wanted to make a place for people to relax, to contemplate, to convalesce, to draw up their own plans of action. In a sense, he wanted to build a memorial to his experience. He asked me to be his architect.

The way that people find faith, I found architecture. Studying the built environment opened my eyes. In architecture school, I began to understand why the world is the way it is. I think of "architecture" as the mystical aspect of the built world—

when a place feels just right — when order is expressed so perfectly that suddenly you become aware of the place where you are. Almost fourteen years after I entered the discipline, I still identify with the language of architecture, how a place silently records a story. I have no architects in my family but somehow I feel it is in my blood. As my father deepens his faith to endure the trials he is facing, I find that I am deepening my faith too, working on a living memorial.

This project turns my mind to other memorials, including one of the first buildings I experienced that, for me, exceeded the definition of "building" and expressed my idea of "architecture." The Women's Memorial and Education Center by Weiss/ Manfredi Architects is a meditation on people and place. Located in Arlington Cemetery and dedicated to all women who served in this country's armed forces, it makes meaning out of the archaeology of its site and the primacy of its larger urban location. Like all good architectural experiences, it invites the visitor to move.

The memorial is dedicated to female soldiers, often forgotten or neglected in the history of national service. To stage the remembrance of these women and their stories, the architects employed a forgotten site: a granite hemicycle located at the end of a drive that reuses the ceremonial gate to Arlington Cemetery, dedicated in 1932 but neglected since. The hemicycle buttresses the cemetery's edge, one story above the entry drive, metaphorically bridging the worlds of the living and the deceased. Across the river from Washington, D.C., it nearly bisects a historic axis between a significant monument and a special gravesite — of two frequently commemorated Presidents, Lincoln and Kennedy. The space behind the hemicycle's stone façade wall was excavated to reveal an existing concrete retaining wall composed of enormous counterforts buttressing the cemetery hillside, with alcoves between. Within these unearthed alcoves, exhibits and archives tell the unearthed stories of female service-women. Sunlight streams into the arc of space between the granite and concrete walls, roofed with glass tablets etched with quotes from these women. Their words cast shadows across the supporting walls below. Visitors commemorate the journey of professional military women by climbing stairs from the entry below, passing through the granite barrier and glass ceiling (pun intended) to a terrace above, where they can view the city and the women's words etched on the tablets. This terrace is an entry porch for Arlington Cemetery.

This memorial was an epiphany to me. The architecture is a structural buttress, a metaphor for the women it commemorates. I always appreciated that the designers asked the participant to dwell upon the subject of the memorial by building a new spatial memory. They also used the telling of a forgotten history of female fighters to whisper a forgotten history of a site, a lost place. In discovering hidden space, I registered a physical interpretation of this place and these voices. The architecture served to remind me of the value of looking beyond the surface. This deepened my understanding in a way that the information in the Education Center did not.

Sometimes the educational aspect of memorials can intrude upon the opportunity to simply dwell in a memory. Equally powerful but characteristically different from the buttressing hemicycle, the buried gash of the Vietnam Veterans memorial has sheer presence to offer a visitor who doesn't take the tour. A Visitors' Center has been proposed, underground, to provide the text and timeline that might be missing upstairs. Critics question how it will disturb the appearance of the memorial. In the context of adjacent corrugated aluminum structures where ice cream and sodas are sold, perhaps the presence of a new building on the landscape is not the issue. Perhaps the question is only whether more text will disturb the integrity of a black stone wall or a simple list of those who fell.

As I design a Center for Meditation, my certainty is less about brick and mortar, more about values. I realize that I know my father's values, but I know nothing about his sense of place, his physical and spatial memories. I once did a painting of our family home in India where he grew up. I sat next to my dad across from the concrete stair that wound up to a single room that his family dedicated for his use only, as the only child of nine to complete college and pursue higher studies. He waxed about how he used to climb that stair every day during medical school and spend the night studying, while the rest of the brood clamored below. As children, my cousins and I competed to see who could jump from the highest step. The low-angled Indian sunlight filtered into the window and cast shadows off each gray step that I watercolored. As I remember the day that I sat next to my dad and sketched, part of me wants to commemorate my father's places in a new architecture.

A particularly heartbreaking memorial that commemorates old places in new architecture is the United States Holocaust Memorial Museum. One room, so wrenching that the path through the exhibits diverges to offer the option of avoiding it, is a railway boxcar. At the time I entered it, I did not know whether it was an actual car used to transport people, or an exact replica. It didn't matter. It was dark. The windows were small. A man next to me broke down. I moved out of there quickly.

My claustrophobia was a type of physical interpretation very different from the one I made passing through the daylit Women's Memorial in Arlington Cemetery. However, it relied just as much on the proportions of a space, lighting, and a path of travel. The claustrophobia came from an architectural experience, but the architecture forced a realization upon me—of the values of a society that allowed a boxcar to mean what it did.

I've never been in a war myself. I find that I depend on architecture for a real sense of what others have experienced. My husband was a child in Dhaka during the Bangladesh war for independence. He tells me about riding an elevator in the city's most posh hotel during a bombing, and stepping into the lobby over a dead body. Somehow that horrific image is too abstract for me to picture, but I can envision it when he describes the carpet, the chandeliers, finishes on the elevator walls. The room has a way of transporting me to the scene.

The day after the 2001 World Trade Center attacks, I did experience what I think is a wartime affectation having nothing to do with buildings, only with people—the hollow stare. For a few days New York was a town of insomniacs with glazed eyes and zombie faces (including my own). It was a profound (and ironically, personal) understanding to share so publicly—with friends, coworkers, firemen, shopkeepers, the mayor. The look is probably common in Gaza or Kashmir. Apart from that insight, my experience of war has been vicarious, made possible only by the foresight of people before me to preserve and consecrate artifacts and significant places. Museum curators argue over how to present—and preserve—a room of shoes or human hair that verify an atrocity. These things speak less to me than spaces that allow me to enter the past. If I can experience the scale of a room with my own body, I can sense its history.

I think that in designing a memorial, encouraging identification in this way might be a method for drawing a participant through a unique experience of the memorial's subject. In the way that the ritual of the Passover Seder encourages the participant to remember not that my ancestors passed through the desert, but that I passed through the desert, the architectural memorial might encourage the visitor to identify with an experience physically, through scale, materiality, shape or subtext of a space. The physical experience translates into an intellectual comprehension, then manifests itself "physically" again in the spatial memory of the participant. I think leaving a visitor with an impression of the memorial's subject is an important way to record and pass on a history.

By this argument, every physical impression at a site contributes to the historical record. Often the art of the impression is more urgent than the details of the events. Adolf Loos, an early Modern architect, speaks of our being able to walk by a place and know that something has happened there:

> *If we find a mound in the forest, six foot long and three foot wide, formed into*
> *a pyramid shape by a shovel, we become serious and something within us says,*
> *'Someone lies buried here'. This is architecture.*
> — Adolf Loos, "Architecture," 1910

Loos' mound in the forest becomes a terrifying architecture if it multiplies into rows and columns of mounds, hundreds of yards long and wide, in the Iraqi desert. To put Loos' observation into a contemporary context, if you drive a jeep to the peak of a dune where you are suddenly afforded a view of the plain below, and you see a great grid of rectangular mounds, clearly arranged into evenly spaced rows and columns, each mound shaped into a pyramid by a hand tool — is that architecture?

Human Rights Watch has been investigating mass graves discovered in Iraq in the last ten years. Filmmakers Kerstin Park-Labella and Buddy Squires recorded a portion of the investigation. Kerstin tells me that as they drive up the hill they aren't expecting to glimpse mass graves; unlike the graves at Arlington Cemetery, these are unanticipated. At the peak, the sudden precise architecture elicits a gasp. The regularity of the composition could only be designed by the human eye.

The mounds of sand could only be manipulated by a shovel held in a human hand—probably the hand of whoever was next in line. Architecture or not, the memory of war is rendered by artifacts like this—mathematical evidence of humans committing atrocities.

The whole point is to dig them up and find an explanation. But these are all organized. Particularly on that side it's row after row almost in a symmetrical fashion and it may be it's not like some of the mass graves that have been found where it's one big pit where a lot of people were machine gunned and buried. This is more systematic and perhaps they may have been added as victims arrived… The stories become physically real in a way because you can see the end results. It's not just words, it's graves.

—Hania Mufti, Human Rights Watch Researcher,
from *Seeking Justice*, Buddy Squires and Kerstin Park-Labella, 2004

Mass graves don't exist for the purpose of memorialization. Their creators never intended to use composition, texture, color, and tectonics to glorify the lives of the inhabitants. In their way, however, they forever alter the perception of a site.

My most recent encounter with a radically altered perception of a site was the World Trade Center site in New York. The firm where I used to work was engaged in a public dialogue that became the design competition for the new building. The two finalists, Daniel Libeskind's firm and the THINK team, differed in approaches to memorialization of the site, though both felt that it was critical that the site itself be allowed to speak.

Libeskind abstracted ideals out of selected physical attributes of the site and manifested abstract ideals into something physical on the site. The shape of the new building was to represent liberty, echoing the view of the Statue of Liberty from the Harbor. The height of the new tower was to equal 1776 feet, to commemorate the year the United States was founded. The slurry wall—the original building foundation and retaining wall for the Hudson River and the only portion of the original towers that remains — was to be exposed, to represent the foundations of democracy. The angle of the sun at the moment of the planes' impact on September 11, 2001, would be manifested physically in the design.

The THINK team reinvented the idea of what the site was for, changing the program from a World Trade Center to a World Cultural Center. The footprint of the two towers became the boundaries for two scaffolds within which anything could be built — performance spaces, parks, community spaces. At night, the skeletal towers would surround two towers of light, the reverse image of the volumes that used to stand there. Sky parks on platforms would be built at the height of the original towers. A funicular would climb up the scaffold, allowing visitors to experience the views and the envelope of the buildings that used to stand on the site.

Both competition entries used the site for vantage. The first proposed commemorating a past moment by investing it with physical form, idealizing the physical and cultural context of the Manhattan site (including New York Harbor and the United States in the definition of the site). The second proposed using the visceral experience of the Manhattan site in the present moment to expand the definition of the site to include the world. The possibility of future developments within the structural frame, the possibility of riding in a funicular and seeing what someone saw on September 10—these things are anchored to the physical experience of a place, while acting as a point of departure for the imagination.

I always liked the THINK solution because it seemed so progressive. I have a bias toward memorials that look forward and subvert the forms we recognize to make new meanings out of events that live vividly in the public imagination. It's such an optimistic approach. When my father acquainted me with his idea for the Center, I felt this same sense of hope about his project. Large sections of the property rendered useless because they would have demanded prohibitively costly building foundations suddenly shined with new character as terraced gardens. The stream that inconveniently cut through the center of the only buildable land would now provide soothing music in this place of repose. This Center would take a disease that we would otherwise like to put behind us and use it to celebrate life.

133

I have been meaning to show my dad another project that inspires me, a monument to anti-fascism by Jochen Gerz and Esther Shalev-Gerz, in Germany. Erected in the center of Harburg, a suburb of Hamburg, on a busy street trafficked by commuters on their way to work, an obelisk with a soft lead surface and attached pencils invites visitors to write. Obelisks were once Roman spoils of war and through time have developed civic associations with town squares. Harburg is a working-class suburb, and the obelisk in this location subverts its counterparts in other European centers by its materiality (soft lead-plated instead of stone), its commercial (rather than civic) site, and its invitation to vandalize.

The project was designed during a time in the last decade when neo-Nazism was on the rise in Western Europe. Visitors were invited to write their names on the sculpture, but the expectation was that graffiti, political slogans, racial slurs—uncensored text from the streets—might find a place on the obelisk. After a head- height of the surfaces of the tall structure filled with words, it was partially sunk into the ground, to clean the slate and invite more writing. In this way, the obelisk endured several sinkings. The project demands that the participant engage, not just in writing on the monument, but in recording history. After its final sinking, this pillar will be gone. The responsibility of keeping the record of injustice lies with us.

As I think about why this monument is meaningful to me, my strongest impression is how ironic it is that although it is meant to disappear, it is most critical that it got built at all. In working on a design project with my dad, the importance of building is what I struggle with most. I sense how difficult it will be for me to work with him. At the moment, our agendas are very different. He needs to keep his mind occupied, and he wants to achieve something tangible quickly. I want, above all, to dwell on getting to know my dad, to spend time figuring out how to put his experience into the ground. I want to make something that will be a historical record, a testament to his life. My approach is probably wrong—too slow for this project—because I don't know how much time we have. I may need to let the site tell me what forms it can bear, rather than trying to get my dad to tell me.

I have begun to think of this project as a memorial to my father's war. I sense that on some level it doesn't matter how we commemorate it, just that we do. I tend to get hung up on finding truthful ways for the design to reflect my dad, but as the poet Anne Sexton put it, "It doesn't matter who my father was; it matters who I remember he was." She had a point. All it took for Loos to find architecture was a mound in the forest. On our site, in our forest, I have been trying to make architecture by making a place for my father, but I think what he really wants is a place for peace.

The Vietnam Memorial in 1987, five years after it was opened.

VIETNAM VETERANS MEMORIAL

by Maya Lin

*It's taken me years to be able to discuss the making of the
Vietnam Veterans Memorial, partly because I needed to move
past it and partly because I had forgotten the process of getting
it built. I would not discuss the controversy surrounding its
construction and it wasn't until I saw the documentary,
Maya Lin: A Strong Clear Vision, that I was able to
remember that time in my life. But I wrote the body of this
essay just as the memorial was being completed—in the fall
of 1982. Then I put it away...until now.*

I think the most important aspect of the design of the *Vietnam Veterans Memorial*
was that I had originally designed it for a class I was taking at Yale and not for the
competition. In that sense, I had designed it for me—or, more exactly, for what I
believed it should be. I never tried to second-guess a jury. And it wasn't until after
I had completed the design that I decided to enter it in the competition.

The design emerged from an architectural seminar I was taking during my senior
year. The initial idea of a memorial had come from a notice posted at the school
announcing a competition for a Vietnam veterans memorial. The class, which was on
funereal architecture, had spent the semester studying how people, through the built
form, express their attitudes on death. As a class, we thought the memorial was an
appropriate design idea for our program, so we adopted it as our final design project.

At that point, not much was known about the actual competition, so for the first half of the assignment we were left without concrete directions as to what "they" were looking for or even who "they" were. Instead, we had to determine for ourselves what a Vietnam memorial should be. Since a previous project had been to design a memorial for World War III, I had already begun to ask the simple questions: What exactly is a memorial? What should it do?

My design for a World War III memorial was a tomblike underground structure that I deliberately made to be a very futile and frustrating experience. I remember the professor of the class, Andrus Burr, coming up to me afterward, saying quite angrily, "If I had a brother who died in that war, I would never want to visit this memorial." I was somewhat puzzled that he didn't quite understand that World War III would be of such devastation that none of us would be around to visit any memorial, and that my design was instead a prewar commentary. In asking myself what a memorial to a third world war would be, I came up with a political statement that was meant as a deterrent.

I had studied earlier monuments and memorials while designing that memorial and I continued this research for the design of the Vietnam memorial. As I did more research on monuments, I realized most carried larger, more general messages about a leader's victory or accomplishments rather than the lives lost. In fact, at the national level, individual lives were very seldom dealt with, until you arrived at the memorials for World War I. Many of these memorials included the names of those killed. Partly it was a practical need to list those whose bodies could not be identified—since dog tags as identification had not yet been adopted and, due to the nature of the warfare, many killed were not identifiable—but I think as well the listing of names reflected a response by these designers to the horrors of World War I, to the immense loss of life.

The images of these monuments were extremely moving. They captured emotionally what I felt memorials should be: honest about the reality of war, about the loss of life in war, and about remembering those who served and especially those who died.

I made a conscious decision not to do any specific research on the Vietnam War and the political turmoil surrounding it. I felt that the politics had eclipsed the veterans, their service and their lives. I wanted to create a memorial that everyone would be able to respond to, regardless of whether one thought our country should or should not have participated in the war. The power of a name was very much with me at the time, partly because of the Memorial Rotunda at Yale. In Woolsey Hall, the walls are inscribed with the names of all the Yale alumni who have been killed in wars. I had never been able to resist touching the names cut into these marble walls, and no matter how busy or crowded the place is, a sense of quiet, a reverence, always surrounds those names. Throughout my freshman and sophomore years, the stonecutters were carving in by hand the names of those killed in the Vietnam War, and I think it left a lasting impression on me. . .the sense of the power of a name.

One memorial I came across also made a strong impression on me. It was a monument to the missing soldiers of the World War I battle of the Somme by Sir Edwin Lutyens in Thiepval, France. The monument includes more than 100,000 names of people who were listed as missing because, without ID tags, it was impossible to identify the dead. (The cemetery contains the bodies of 70,000 dead.) To walk past those names and realize those lost lives—the effect of that is the strength of the design. This memorial acknowledged those lives without focusing on the war or on creating a political statement of victory or loss. This apolitical approach became the essential aim of my design; I did not want to civilize war by glorifying it or by forgetting the sacrifices involved. The price of a human life in war should always be clearly remembered.

But on a personal level, I wanted to focus on the nature of accepting and coming to terms with a loved one's death. Simple as it may seem, I remember feeling that accepting a person's death is the first step in being able to overcome that loss.

I felt that as a culture we were extremely youth-oriented and not willing or able to accept death or dying as a part of life. The rites of mourning, which in more primitive and older cultures were very much a part of life, have been suppressed in our modern times. In the design of the memorial, a fundamental goal was to be honest

MAYA LIN

about death, since we must accept that loss in order to begin to overcome it. The pain of the loss will always be there, it will always hurt, but we must acknowledge the death in order to move on.

What then would bring back the memory of a person? A specific object or image would be limiting. A realistic sculpture would be only one interpretation of that time. I wanted something that all people could relate to on a personal level. At this time I had as yet no form, no specific artistic image.

The use of names was a way to bring back everything someone could remember about a person. The strength in a name is something that has always made me wonder at the "abstraction" of the design; the ability of a name to bring back every single memory you have of that person is far more realistic and specific and much more comprehensive than a still photograph, which captures a specific moment in time or a single event or a generalized image that may or may not be moving for all who have connections to that time.

Then someone in the class received the design program, which stated the basic philosophy of the memorial's design and also its requirements: all the names of those missing and killed (57,000) must be part of the memorial; the design must be apolitical, harmonious with the site, and conciliatory.

These were all the thoughts that were in my mind before I went to see the site.

Without having seen it, I couldn't design the memorial, so a few of us traveled to Washington, D.C., and it was at the site that the idea for the design took shape. The site was a beautiful park surrounded by trees, with traffic and noise coming from one side—Constitution Avenue.

I had a simple impulse to cut into the earth.

I imagined taking a knife and cutting into the earth, opening it up, an initial violence and pain that in time would heal. The grass would grow back, but the initial cut would remain a pure flat surface in the earth with a polished, mirrored surface, much like the surface on a geode when you cut it and polish the edge. The need for the names to be on the memorial would become the memorial; there was no need to embellish the design further. The people and their names would allow everyone to respond and remember.

It would be an interface, between our world and the quieter, darker, more peaceful world beyond. I chose black granite in order to make the surface reflective and peaceful. I never looked at the memorial as a wall, an object, but as an edge to the earth, an opened side. The mirrored effect would double the size of the park, creating two worlds, one we are a part of and one we cannot enter. The two walls were positioned so that one pointed to the Lincoln Memorial and the other pointed to the Washington Monument. By linking these two strong symbols for the country, I wanted to create a unity between the nation's past and present.

The idea of destroying the park to create something that by its very nature should commemorate life seemed hypocritical, nor was it in my nature. I wanted my design to work with the land, to make something with the site, not to fight it or dominate it. I see my works and their relationship to the landscape as being an additive rather than a combative process.

On our return to Yale, I quickly sketched my idea up, and it almost seemed too simple, too little. I toyed with adding some large flat slabs that would appear to lead into the memorial, but they didn't belong. The image was so simple that anything added to it began to detract from it.

———

I always wanted the names to be chronological, to make it so that those who served and returned from the war could find their place in the memorial. I initially had the names beginning on the left side and ending on the right. In a preliminary critique, a professor asked what importance that left for the apex, and I, too, thought it was a weak point, so I changed the design for the final critique. Now the chronological sequence began and ended at the apex so that the time line would circle back to itself and close the sequence. A progression in time is memorialized. The design is not just a list of the dead. To find one name, chances are you will see the others close by, and you will see yourself reflected through them.

The memorial was designed before I decided to enter the competition. I didn't even consider that it might win. When I submitted the project, I had the greatest difficulty trying to describe it in just one page. It took longer, in fact, to write the

MAYA LIN

statement that I felt was needed to accompany the required drawings than to design the memorial. The description was critical to understanding the design since the memorial worked more on an emotional level than a formal level.

Coincidentally, at the time, I was taking a course with Professor Vincent Scully, in which he just happened to focus on the same memorial I had been so moved by— the Lutyens memorial to the missing. Professor Scully described one's experience of that piece as a passage or journey through a yawning archway. As he described it, it resembled a gaping scream, which after you passed through, you were left looking out on a simple graveyard with the crosses and tombstones of the French and the English. It was a journey to an awareness of immeasurable loss, with the names of the missing carved on every surface of this immense archway.

—ɯ—

I started writing furiously in Scully's class. I think he has always been puzzled by my connection to the Lutyens memorial. Formally the two memorials could not be more different. But for me, the experiences of these two memorials describe a similar passage to an awareness about loss.

The competition required drawings, along with the option to include a written description. As the deadline for submission approached, I created a series of simple drawings. The only thing left was to complete the essay, which I instinctively knew was the only way to get anyone to understand the design, the form of which was deceptively simple. I kept reworking and reediting the final description. I actually never quite finished it. I ended up at the last minute writing freehand directly onto the presentation boards (you can see a few misprints on the actual page), and then I sent the project in, never expecting to hear about it again.

The drawings were in soft pastels, very mysterious, very painterly, and not at all typical of architectural drawings. One of the comments made by a juror was "*He* must really know what he is doing to dare to do something so naïve" (italics mine). But ultimately, I think it was the written description that convinced the jurors to select my design.

On my last day of classes my roommate, Liz Perry, came to retrieve me from one of my classes, telling me a call from Washington had come in and that it was from the Vietnam Veterans Memorial Fund; they needed to talk to me and would call back with a few questions about the design. When they called back, they merely said they needed to ask me a few questions and wanted to fly up to New Haven to talk to me. I was convinced that I was number 100 and they were only going to question me about drainage and other technical issues. It never occurred to me that I might have won the competition. It was still, in my mind, an exercise—as competitions customarily are for architecture students.

And even after three officers of the fund were seated in my college dorm room, explaining to me that it was the largest competition of its kind, with more than fourteen hundred entries, and Colonel Schaet, who was talking, without missing a beat calmly added that I had won (I think my roommate's face showed more emotion than mine did at the time), it still hadn't registered. I don't think it did for almost a year. Having studied the nature of competitions, especially in Washington (for instance, the F.D.R. Memorial, still unbuilt in 1981, nearly forty years after it was first proposed, or the artwork Robert Venturi and Richard Serra collaborated on for L'Enfant Plaza, which was completely modified as it went through the required Washington design process of approvals), my attitude about unusual projects getting built in Washington was not optimistic. Partly it's my nature—I never get my hopes up—and partly I assumed the simplicity of the design, and its atypical form and color, would afford it a difficult time through the various governmental-approval agencies.

After the design had been chosen, it was subject to approval by various governmental agencies at both the conceptual and design development phases. I moved to Washington and stayed there throughout these phases. I expected the design to be debated within the design-approval agencies; I never expected the politics that constantly surrounded its development and fabrication.

I was driven down to D.C. the day of my college graduation, and I immediately became part of an internal struggle for the control of the design. I think my age made it seem apparent to some that I was too young to understand what I had done or to see it through to completion. To bring the design into reality would require that I associate with an architect of record, a qualified firm that would work with me to

143

realize the design. I had a very difficult time convincing the fund in charge of the memorial, the V.V.M.F., of the importance of selecting a qualified firm that had experience both in architecture and landscape-integrated solutions, and that would be sympathetic to the design.

I had gone to Cesar Pelli, then dean of Yale's School of Architecture, for the names of some firms that could handle the job. A firm by the name of Cooper-Lecky was the one he recommended, and I presented its name to the fund, unaware that the competition's adviser was the fund's choice as architect of record. I was told by the fund that this person was the architect of record, and that was that.

After a few weeks of tense and hostile negotiations (in which at one point I was warned that I would regret these actions, and that I would "come crawling back on my hands and knees"), I was finally able to convince the fund to go through a legitimate process of selecting a firm to become the architect of record. The then architecture critic for the *Washington Post*, Wolf Von Eckhardt, was instrumental in pressing the fund to listen to me. But the struggle left a considerable amount of ill will and mistrust between the veterans and myself.

Through the remaining phases of the project I worked with the Cooper-Lecky architectural firm. We worked on the practical details of the design, from the addition of a safety curb to a sidewalk to the problems in inscribing the names. Many of the issues we dealt with were connected to the text and my decision to list the names chronologically. People felt it would be an inconvenience to have to search out a name in a book and then find its panel location and thought that an alphabetical listing would be more convenient—until a tally of how many Smiths had died made it clear that an alphabetical listing wouldn't be feasible. The M.I.A. groups wanted their list of the missing separated out and listed alphabetically. I knew this would break the strength of the time line, interrupting the real-time experience of the piece, so I fought hard to maintain the chronological listing. I ended up convincing the groups that the time in which an individual was noted as missing was the emotionally compelling time for family members. A system of noting these names with a symbol* that could be modified to signify if the veteran was later found alive or officially declared dead would appease the concerns of the M.I.A. groups without breaking the time line. I knew the time line was key to the experience of the memorial: a returning veteran would be able to find his or her time of service when finding a friend's name.

The text of the memorial and the fact that I had left out everything except the names led to a fight as to what else needed to be said about the war. The apex is the memorial's strongest point; I argued against the addition of text at that point for fear that a politically charged statement, one that would force a specific reading, would destroy the apolitical nature of the design. Throughout this time I was very careful not to discuss my beliefs in terms of politics; I played it extremely naïve about politics, instead turning the issue into a strictly aesthetic one. Text could be added, but what-ever was said needed to fit in three lines—to match the height of the dates "1959" and "1975" that it would be adjacent to. The veterans approved this graphic parameter, and the statements became a simple prologue and epilogue.

The memorial is analogous to a book in many ways. Note that on the right-hand panels the pages are set ragged right and on the left they are set ragged left, creating a spine at the apex as in a book. Another issue was scale; the text type is the smallest that we had come across, less than half an inch, which is unheard of in monument type sizing. What it does is create a very intimate reading in a very public space, the difference in intimacy between reading a billboard and reading a book.

The only other issue was the polished black granite and how it should be detailed, over which I remember having a few arguments with the architects of record. The architects could not understand my choice of a reflective, highly polished black granite. One of them felt I was making a mistake and the polished surface would be "too feminine." Also puzzling to them was my choice of detailing the monument as a thin veneer with barely any thickness at its top edge. They wanted to make the monument's walls read as a massive, thick stone wall, which was not my intention at

---

* Each name is preceded (on the west wall) or followed (on the east wall) by one of two symbols: a diamond or a cross. The diamond denotes that the serviceman's or servicewoman's death was confirmed. The cross symbolizes those who were missing in action or prisoners at the end of the war. When a serviceperson's remains were returned, the diamond symbol is superimposed over the cross. If a serviceman or woman returns alive, a circle will be inscribed around the cross.

MAYA LIN

all. I always saw the wall as pure surface, an interface between light and dark, where I cut the earth and polished its open edge. The wall dematerializes as a form and allows the names to become the object, a pure and reflective surface that would allow visitors the chance to see themselves with the names. I do not think I thought of the color black as a color, more as the idea of a dark mirror into a shadowed mirrored image of the space, a space we cannot enter and from which the names separate us, an interface between the world of the living and the world of the dead.

—◊◊◊—

One aspect that made the project unusual was its politicized building process. For instance, the granite could not come from Canada or Sweden. Though those countries had beautiful black granites, draft evaders went to both countries, so the veterans felt that we could not consider their granites as options. (The stone finally selected came from India.) The actual building process went smoothly for the most part, and the memorial was built very close to my original intentions.

As far as all of the controversy, I really never wanted to go into it too much. The memorial's starkness, its being below grade, being black, and how much my age, gender, and race played a part in the controversy, we'll never quite know. I think it is actually a miracle that the piece ever got built. From the very beginning I often wondered, if it had not been an anonymous entry 1026 but rather an entry by Maya Lin, would I have been selected?

I remember at the very first press conference a reporter asking me if I did not find it ironic that the memorial was for the Vietnam War and that I was of Asian descent. I was so righteous in my response that my race was completely irrelevant. It took me almost nine months to ask the V.V.M.F., in charge of building the memorial, if my race was at all an issue. It had never occurred to me that it would be, and I think they had taken all the measures they could to shield me from such comments about a "gook" designing the memorial.

I remember reading an article that appeared in the *Washington Post* referring to "An Asian Memorial for an Asian War" and I knew we were in trouble. The controversy exploded in Washington after that article. Ironically, one side attacked the design for being "too Asian," while others saw its simplicity and understatement, not as an intention to create a more Eastern, meditative space, but as a minimalist statement which they interpreted as being non-referential and disconnected from human experience.

This left the opinion in many that the piece emanated from a series of intellectualized aesthetic decisions, which automatically pitted artist against veterans. The fact that I was from an Ivy League college, had hair down to my knees, further fueled this distrust of the design and suspicions of a hippie college liberal or aesthetic elitist forcing her art and commentary upon them.

Perhaps it was an empathetic response to the idea about war that had led me to cut open the earth—an initial violence that heals in time but leaves a memory, like a scar. But this imagery, which some detractors would later describe as "a black gash of shame and sorrow" in which the color black was called the "universal color of shame and dishonor," would prove incredibly difficult to defend. The misreading of the design as a negative political statement that in some ways was meant to reflect upon the service of the veterans was in part fueled by a cultural prejudice against the color black as well as by the misreading or misinformation that led some veterans to imagine the design as a ditch or a hole. It took a prominent four-star general, Brigadier General George Price, who happened to be black, testifying before one of the countless subcommittee hearings and defending the color black, before the design could move forward.

But the distrust, the fact that no veterans had been on the jury, the unconventionality of the design and the designer, and a very radical requirement made by the Vietnam veterans to include all the names of those killed made it inevitable that the project would become controversial. I think ultimately that much of the negative response goes back to the very natural response to cover up or not acknowledge that which is painful or unpleasant. The very fact that the veterans themselves had required the listing and therefore the acknowledgement of the more than 57,000 casualties, which is a landmark in our country in terms of seeing a war via the individual lives lost, was very hard for many to face. I remember Ross Perot when he was trying to persuade the veterans that it was an inappropriate design, asking me if I truly didn't feel that the veterans would prefer a parade instead, something happy or uplifting, and I can remember thinking that a parade would not in the long term help them overcome the enormous trauma of the politics of that war.

I do not think I fully realized until the dedication and homecoming parade that the veterans needed both. In effect the veterans gave themselves their own homecoming. In November 1982, I was in tears watching these men welcoming themselves home after almost ten years of not being acknowledged by their country for their service, their sacrifice.

But until the memorial was built I don't think they realized that the design was experiential and cathartic, and, most importantly, designed not for me, but for them. They didn't see that the chronology of the names allowed a returning veteran the ability to find his or her own time frame on the wall and created a psychological space for them that directly focused on human response and feeling. I remember one of the veterans asking me before the wall was built what I thought people's reaction would be to it. I realized then that these veterans were willing to defend a design they really didn't quite understand. I was too afraid to tell him what I was thinking, that I knew a returning veteran would cry.

An architect once told me to look always at what was originally envisioned and try to keep it. I left Washington before ground breaking. I had to. The fund and I knew that we had to accept a compromise. The closer you watch something grow, the less able you are to notice changes in it. When I saw the site again, the granite panels were being put up and the place was frighteningly close to what I thought it should be. It terrified me. It was a strange feeling, to have had an idea that was solely yours be no longer a part of your mind but totally public, no longer yours.

There was always the expectation that since the war had been controversial, the memorial must be also. It wasn't so much an artistic dispute as a political one. The choice to make an apolitical memorial was in itself political to those who felt only a positive statement about the war would make up for the earlier antiwar days, a past swing to the left now to be balanced. It was extremely naïve of me to think that I could produce a neutral statement that would not become politically controversial simply because it chose not to take sides.

Anyway, the push, as one congressman put it, to "politicize" the design didn't really affect the memorial in this way. The addition of the statue of infantrymen and then the addition of the female statue to make them equal are to me sad indicators that some politicians believe that you can please all of the people all of the time by compromise and conglomerate works. These statues leave only the false reading that the wall is for the dead and they are for the living, when the design I made was for the returning veterans and equally names all who served regardless of race, creed, or sex. I am only glad that the three infantrymen are not where they had been originally intended, right in the center of the memorial, heads sticking up higher than the walls, converting the walls to a backdrop and violating that private contemplative space. Ironically, the compromise memorializes the conflict in the building of the piece.

People cannot resolve that war, nor can they separate the issues, the politics, from it. As for me, the first time I visited the memorial after it was completed I found myself searching out the name of a friend's father and touching it. It was strange to realize that I was another visitor and I was reacting to it as I had designed it.

RECOVERIES

The author's grandfather, David Canicosa.

MEDITATIONS ON AN OLD LOVE, ENSHROUDED IN PRAYER

by Michael Sandoval

We wonder at this: a man in a white suit holds a white hat, arms held at his sides, palm trees and a *calesa*, a horse-drawn carriage, just out of focus in the background. Where the picture was taken we don't know—Hong Kong, perhaps, maybe Manila Bay. He is a dapper-looking man of about thirty—hair combed back with Pomade, his body frozen into one of those half-awkward poses we stiffen into while waiting for the camera to flash. The picture was taken around 1936. His name is David Canicosa, on a trip to buy cloth for a small store he runs in Manila. He waits patiently in the hot, equatorial sun, even as the Pomade melts and his skin sweats in his white cotton suit.

The framed black-and-white photo sits on a shelf in my sister's house in Long Island, hidden between a miniature Zen rock garden and a Jets souvenir football. If you were to pluck this photo from the frame and look at the back, you would discover a note written in the neat, elegant script people used before fountain pens became museum pieces. *"My Dear Felising, / Who is this handsome man?"* signs David. *"Whoever he is,"* he concludes, *"he is thinking of you."*

David falls deeply in love with the woman to whom the photograph is dedicated: a young schoolteacher nicknamed Felising, née Felisa Saguil. They marry and have five children. Five years after the photo is taken, a war comes to their doorstep. One child is lost. On an unknown date in 1945, the door to his house is broken down by soldiers of the Japanese Imperial Army. In front of his wife, David is dragged away into the night.

I can't remember the first time I saw the photo, or when my sister discovered it and framed it as her own. I believe that the woman, Felisa, my grandmother, kept this photo hidden through my childhood years. I recall being told at an early age that there existed this man, this ghost, whose name I inherited (my middle name being David). Not much else was revealed.

To look at this photograph means to tread upon the grey line between memory and sentimentality: to enter into the soft-edged space of childhood; of apparitions glimpsed through half-opened doors. Children are empathic creatures, whose aptitude for recollection favors the extremes. To be raised by a war survivor means to live immersed in an acute dichotomy of tenderness and grief. It is an experience at once comforting and extraordinarily confusing.

I am haunted by an image: Felisa Canicosa is seventy years old, folding clothes in front of the television. I am a young child, poking my head into the family room. The din of a game show plays in the background. Glass patio doors open up to a garden and a stone landing. Light streams onto the orange carpet. It is August in Michigan, and the leaves in full spread are brushing against the glass doors.

On Halloween, she hands out fistfuls of candy to the neighborhood kids, for which she develops a great and admiring reputation. Despite her seventy-plus years, she spends much of the fall raking and bagging leaves. On a trip to Disneyland, Felisa, now stricken with arthritis, is left on a bench while my sisters and I scamper off to the rides. We return hours later when dusk has fallen. Her frown betrays a sense of uselessness, but she sits upright and undefeated, like a shopping bag unwilling to admit it is forgotten. On a road trip in the early '80s, someone slams the van door onto her finger, crushing it into gel. She displays no signs of pain.

We do not call her "Grandma" or the Filipino "lola," but "Mama," pronounced with a soft *a*: "Mum-mah:" A quiet but resilient sound, good for the cook, the nurturer, the gardener, the disciplinarian of the house. I hear sounds of slapping. I am nine, and Mama is coaxing me to play piano with the help of a rubber slipper judiciously applied to my behind. She orders me to scrape coconuts for a Sunday meal; to dust, to mop by placing rags on my feet and dancing. One summer, a friend drops a 2x4 on my face; my grandmother bandages the cut and saves the eye.

There is an aura about her. Air thick with the existence of something else hovering around the house's walls. As warm as she can be, as generous as she is with food heaped on a grandchild's plate, she remains estranged from the outside world by an indecipherable solemnity hinting of fatalism and Catholicism and the afterlife. She prays—always. She does not seek companionship. Never once does a visitor call, or a friend stop by. She gardens and cooks and raises the grandchildren in relative silence for twenty-five years. She nails a cross to the front door and a three-foot statue of Jesus above the stairs.

The haunting scene returns. I am a seven-year-old boy, peering into a family room. There is an old woman ironing quietly, the television droning on. Bob Barker is calming another screaming contestant. I pause, for a moment. The scene seems idyllic, but something is not quite right. The iron's movement is erratic. Her arm is trembling, slightly, and her eyes are closed. For some mystifying reason, she is crying.

She is always crying, I realize. Alone in her room, in the bathroom, head bowed. On her bed, in front of her altar. Clasping a prayer, shaking—in church, in her room in the evenings, on the couch when no one is around. Hands clasped, head pressed against the hands.

For twenty-five years, I grow up watching a tough, beloved old woman lapse into spontaneous and inexplicable moments of grief, as if someone just passed away that morning. The discomfort a seven year old feels can be as awesome as his own lack of understanding of mortality. As a child, I walk up and pull on a sleeve—"What's wrong?" I ask. To my eternal frustration, nobody ever says.

Mama lives almost three decades in a suburb of Detroit. Never once does she mention David Canicosa by her own accord. The word "atrocity" is something I first learn in high school, in history books on the Holocaust or Vietnam. My sisters and I find out about his existence through fragments of sentences whispered to us with trepidation by relatives. "Ay nako! What she went through!" they exclaim, their voices trailing off. We, as children, try to reconcile this statement with the woman making Spam sandwiches and fried bananas for lunch, and we scratch our heads and ponder. Years and years will pass before I have the wherewithal to knit together textbook history with the jumbled fragments of recollection.

I imagine Manila in February, 1945. Within the city limits, the Japanese military is on a rampage. Men and women and children are being chased down and shot. Caught between the artillery shells of one army and the machine guns of another, the inhabitants of the city pray and huddle in the ruins. The Americans seem frenzied by the taste of victory, colonial masters of the Philippines reclaiming a lost prize. The Japanese army, deposed colonial masters, are likewise crazed, in this case by the reality of their impending defeat.

In between these colliding forces, Felisa and David Canicosa shelter their children in the back room of their house. Shrapnel explodes in the corridor. Felisa glimpses soldiers dying through the foyer window. Together they construct a barricade against the door. The soldiers break it down. David is knocked to the floor, where he is kicked and prodded with rifle butts. I don't know if Felisa clings to a soldier's arm, or whether something unspeakable is done to her. My mother is too young to remember. My grandmother is not. She sees her husband dragged into the street. The door is an empty space: wood off the hinges, blackness and fires.

Felisa gathers her children, and they sneak out the back. There is a crack in the high stone wall outside (my aunt, Tita Josie, recollects). Felisa scrapes the bricks until her fingers bleed and squeezes four daughters and an adopted son through. The oldest is twelve, the youngest, my mother, barely four years old. They escape into an open field. Then there is no more running. The night becomes lit by fire and explosions.

Old tragedies have no place in the prosperity of immigrants, especially of their children. We are raised as if a veil has been drawn between the past and the present. The comfortable house we inhabit—all signs seem to say—has been won precisely because the limitations of the past have been overcome. Yet we know as children that there once existed this man who is now dead—indeed, the voices whisper, who was murdered, whose body was found, they say, in a puddle. I know I am named after him. On our first pilgrimage to the Philippines, my sisters and I even visit his headstone. We do not know yet that there is no body beneath it, that he is buried in some unmarked mass grave. We live a rosy life in a wooded suburb in Michigan, ensconced in the resonance of a history inextricably linked not just to a textbook snapshot but to the hand that once fed us, now so stricken with arthritis it can barely hold the missalette shielding wet eyes from prying churchgoers.

This is what it means to inherit war. To have etched into summer memories of building tree forts and my first Star Wars figures, the image of an old woman wrapped in incense, convulsing. Her entreaties to God filling the ambience of a kitchen. I fall asleep with prayers ringing the edges of my ears.

"Oh! Most sacred heart of Jesus, fountain of every blessing, I adore thee, I love thee. And with a lively sorrow for my sins, I offer thee this poor heart of mine."
I inculcate these prayers. Thirty years later, I still remember them by heart. I repeat them constantly. Not just in prayer sessions with her, but on my bed in the middle of the night, in the first hours of the morning before the sun comes up. One summer I become so enraptured with the prayers that my friends at camp think that I've gone bonkers, always talking to myself. My parents are convinced I will become a priest. These misinterpretations are embarrassing, but I continue for fear of breaking some sort of sacred trust.

I am bound by the pallor of a secret: a double bed in my grandmother's room with one side always empty. I become part of this mystery. Discomfort in the house is fact, like wallpaper or the way glass fogs when one breathes too closely. Something else hovers there, nameless as the ghost in the closet at night.

—⁂—

That evening, Manila is ripped apart by a savage artillery bombardment by the Americans, who seem to have forgotten that allied civilians live in the city. The field where Felisa has fled shelters hundreds of families, huddled in clumps like moles driven from their holes. She pulls the bullet-ridden mattress over her children. Every now and then, a family next to Felisa is hit. This is the cycle: the cry of the hurtling

MICHAEL SANDOVAL

shell; the screams of a family and the explosion; the raining down of earth and charred flesh. Then the infinitesimal space of silence before the cycle repeats again, for an endless night.

Around Felisa and the children, neighbors evaporate into the air. Sensations become compressed into a long and constant shrill, and fires burn in a ring from the fallen timbers of the buildings.

We are the grandchildren of those who suffered through war, and we inherit pain: in our confusion, in our unabashed empathy, in our powerlessness. We are oblivious to the details, but we are full of questions. Why? When? Who? How? No answer is given. We are left to blithely accept our ignorance, taking stabs to guess. (Wasn't she ever happy, here in the Promised Land, this green Michigan landscape?) We troll this strange phenomenon of memory and procure bits.

So here is what I re-imagine, culled from snippets of overheard conversations and furtive interviews in the din dark of a sala in Quezon City. I see the morning, the air is torpid: heat from the unforgiving equatorial sun; heat emanating from the ground; heat from the gases and smoke. The field is a mush of bodies and muck made of flesh. The air smells of cordite, and flies have come out. Felisa gathers her children. She can barely stand. She has been sick for weeks with pneumonia, which killed her two-year-old son a few months before. She knows she is going to die. She dusts her children off and says goodbye, telling them to follow her twelve-year-old adopted son down a set of railroad tracks. If they stick to the tracks, they will reach, God help them, a relative's house. (Which relative? I ask Mama once. She can't recall.) She is too weak to fight her impulses. She breathes because of a single goal: she herself must leave and find her husband.

This is what my aunt, Tita Josie, tells me, who was nine years old when her mother pushed her away. The batteries of my tape recorder have died, and I have to scribble furiously. Tita Josie fans herself in her sala in her house in Quezon City. *We were just four,* Tita Josie says. *Four girls following your Tito Tony single file back to the house.* She continues: *There were so many bodies. My god we had to step on them.*

And she pauses.

It was so hard on her, she says, finally. *Sobra naman. I don't want to remember...*
And she drifts off.

Recollections become metaphors. Select images come to stand for the infinite moment. I see an old woman rocking in prayer in front of *The Price is Right*; my grandmother shifts through her own pictures.

I have walked down Manila streets during the hot season, when the humidity melts the garbage and makes the sweat stink on the skin. Felisa walks through such heat with the stench of a thousand corpses wafting up. They distract her no more than rocks or litter on a road. She has a singular intention, which is to appease the nagging ache and gnawing panic trying to burst from her ribs.

To the left, the gutted shells of houses; to the right, columns of smoke turning the horizon into an acrid yellow. Under her feet crunch the rubble of exploded concrete and glass, twisted limbs and carbonized bodies. And in the distance, something that seems, at first, a miracle, but then slowly something else. Because she finds David, hope out of hope. He is lying face down in a puddle. And he is dead. (This is the version first whispered to my sisters and me. Other relatives say he was found in a ditch along with some other bodies. My grandmother's younger sister, whom I interview in 1992, says he was floating in a lily pond.) Felisa recognizes David from the hundreds of corpses around him by the rosary around his neck. The bloodstains indicate that he was bayoneted in the back.

When she rolls his sodden body from the water, does she recoil from the horror of this desecration? Or does she catch, during a fleeting moment of precognition, a glimpse of the long years without him? My aunts say that their mother lifts the body to her back and begins to half-drag, half-carry it home. She walks for miles. The body is fetid and heavy. Pneumonia makes each step difficult. She has not had a drink of water for two days.

Another relative says that after hours she grows exhausted, stumbles and lays the body down. She begs some people to bury it, paying them all the money she has remaining. The people run off with the money. Everybody is in agreement that an American army truck drives past. Whether she flags it down or whether the soldiers

159

stop and compel her to hand over the body, nobody knows. Probably there were dozens of trucks moving through the ruins, their flatbeds overflowing with the dead. What we know is that David, the man of the pressed, white linen suit, is thrown onto a heap of corpses on the truck and is not seen again.

— ∿ —

I take a picture of Felisa in 1992, the year she knows she is going to die. She is resting her chin on her palm behind a table. In front of her sits a potted orchid. Soft light is coming in through a window, like a Jan Vermeer painting. She is tense, as if she is trying to contain a stomachache. I have just driven her to dialysis—a painful experience, to have your kidneys emptied by a machine. I interview her on tape.

"Where did he work, Mama?" I ask. *"How did you meet? Where was your house in Manila?"*

I glean the thinnest of information. Her answers become curt, taper into half-finished sentences. I cajole her to answer.

"I don't want!" she cries, looking exhausted. "My head hurts. Your questions give me a headache." She massages her temples. The tape recorder hisses for a few moments, then stops.

When the war ends, she survives by teaching English to Chinese immigrants to Manila, who in gratitude give her two gold necklaces, one of which is snatched on a jeepney. She works, hard, hard; up at dawn, teaching, scrimping, saving. A widow in a city leveled by the war, she works hard enough to feed and clothe her children. They all go to university. In 1963, her youngest completes medical school and immigrates to the States. This daughter finishes residency in Syracuse and moves to Detroit and marries my father. In 1966, Felisa immigrates to the U.S. and joins them.

My father confides that her care for us children allowed him and my mother to keep their jobs. He tells me that she used to massage my stomach when I was a baby to ease my digestion problems. In the '70s she is still robust: cuts brambles and digs holes in soil; folds each article of clothing in impeccable squares; sews by hand. She defines herself by the work. In 1988, she cradles one hand in the other. Her hands are riddled with arthritis. She can only curl the fingertips. "This is as tight as I can close it," she says to no one in particular.

She places a thousand rosaries about our house. Ones made of compressed roses. Glow-in-the dark ones; rosaries of beautiful silver spheres and ones of cheap pink plastic. Laminated prayers are wrapped in hair bands and placed in stacks inside a drawer smelling of Tiger Balm. In her room, Mama dusts an elaborate altar laid on lace cloth. Candles stand a foot high: some on brass candlesticks, one blessed by the Pope. Statues of the Virgin Mary, Jesus Christ, St. Joseph, and the Santo Niño rise up on wooden pedestals. Over the mirror hangs another rosary the cross of which is longer than my arm, with wooden beads the size of golf balls. The smell of jasmine wafts out from a Chinese incense burner. To the side is a portrait of Jesus that lights up from a bulb in the back. Mama's sense of contrition is inescapable. *"...And with a lively sorrow for our sins,"* she whispers, *"...we offer thee these poor hearts of ours."* My sisters and I kneel on the carpeted floor next to my grandmother until the candles burn low.

A photo is kept hidden in a drawer. A man stands and smiles in his awkward pose for eternity. Stories are told. Children are raised. Countless prayers are recited. Tons of clothes ironed, a million pots washed.

She can't make a fist. She sits there, staring at her hand: opening, closing; opening, closing. When the hands stiffen and lose their ability to cook, knit, hoe, feed, polish, chop; when there are no more children to take care of because they have gone to college and left, she sits in front of an orchid for hours, alone with her thoughts.

It has been said that Filipinos, with their long history of contending with smug occupiers—Spanish, American, and Japanese—resist by bending but keeping their feet on the ground and living for the next day. The proverbial cliché of strength in the Orient. What is repeated less often is that to be kept constantly at a bend is extraordinarily taxing. Survivors of atrocities have the double burden of surviving the act of surviving.

MICHAEL SANDOVAL

She drops hints of her own impending death a decade before she passes away. "I'm going to die," she says when I am thirteen. I have no idea what to make of this. "I'll be looking down on you," she says. "I'll be a ghost. I'll sneak up behind and *kurot* (pinch) you!"

A U.S. army truck pulls away in a cloud of dust. She is placed in a hospital, where the doctors predict she will die the next day. The nurses mull over kicking her off the bed, to make room for the sick lining the corridors who have a real chance to live. Felisa awakens at night to find a Holy Scapula and a rosary on the foot of her bed. In her feverish state, she prays the rosary. The doctors come to her bed the next morning, expecting to find a corpse. Instead, they discover a woman gently breathing beneath the sheets. The doctors and nurses are astonished. "It's a miracle!" they whisper. (Our genesis in this country—predicated not just in tragedy but in faith and enigma.) But a war has just ended and a city destroyed, and a hundred thousand people killed. They move on.

And forty years pass by.

In 1992, Felisa is flown back to Manila during the last months she is alive, because she wants to be buried next to the headstone of her husband. During her funeral, her girls, now middle-aged, whisper in awe of her stamina. She can't be buried next to her husband's headstone because of flooding problems at the cemetery. She is laid to rest in a graveyard in Quezon City during a rainy afternoon. I give a eulogy, and get criticized because I keep my hands in my pockets like an awkward schoolboy. A year later, a photo is found and framed.

Felisa has just injected herself with insulin. I am an adult, watching her from across the table. She needs two hands to haul herself up the three steps from the foyer to the kitchen. I follow her behind on the steps, to catch her in case she falls. She opens her pillbox and begins the half-hour ritual of ingesting twenty-five pills. She shuts her eyes, for a moment.

Is it a kiss in Luneta Park that she remembers? Of David pressing the feverish body of his son to his chest under a mosquito net on a humid night? Does she remember a man in a white suit who tilts his hat over his eyes to look more dashing? Does she recall the fights that were never resolved? A gift of a flower? She recollects the guava tree and the blossoms of the plants in front of their first home. She recalls selling the house to a duplicitous relative during the war, who refuses to pay with anything but Philippine Japanese currency, worthless. She remembers a ring—stolen; a property deed—pilfered from a box by another relative. She remembers the arms of a man who held her while a city burned around her.

She is dreaming, and we are dreaming. There is my grandfather, younger than I, posing for a postcard snapshot before he rushes off for a meeting. In the background drifts a Cole Porter tune from somebody's old Victrola, the music drifting through a second floor shutter, down past the palms through the humid sea air. There is Felisa, an old, arthritic woman who dyes black her white hair, who smells of Ben Gay and Tiger Balm, who stops while ironing clothes for a moment too long to call a pause. There she is, a young woman coughing on a balcony, holding a postcard to the light, imagining the shape of this man as if he were close enough for her to taste his breath. Only this broken moment of an image to be lived again and again.

The author's grandparents' wedding photo.

BROKEN PIECES

by Jennifer F. Estaris

I

My parents never told me any stories, and I never found it appropriate or necessary
to ask. Here and there, I would hear delicate fragments of a past life. I have all these
shattered bits, but I have never been able to piece together a coherent, linear tale.
The man and woman who were to become my parents left the Philippines after
college, the new world holding no memories. My father intended to return home after
finishing his medical residency in Chicago; instead, he married a beautiful Filipina
nurse and settled down in a cozy Baltimore suburb.

The past was difficult to piece together. When my grandparents visited, nothing
they did made any sense. I found old age implausible. I seldom conversed with anyone
older than sixty. I avoided the elderly, as though their rusty spirits were contagious.
I grew up in a young city, an Atlanta recreated after the Civil War. In contrast, old
age and antiquities seemed bewildering. Or maybe I found old age mystifying because
I didn't know my grandparents well, even though they visited us from the Philippines.
Old people, as I knew them, did not have pasts. They began old.

"Papa" and "Mama" would stay in the house and, as it seemed to me, wander
around. At the break of dawn, they were already up, cooking *almusal*, breakfast.
Usually they made sweet and salty sausages, *longaniza*, or a sweet cured pork, *tocino*.

These meats were laid on a plate covered with a paper towel alongside a bowl of yesterday's rice, fried simply with garlic. If the savory smell did not wake me from my dreams, the zip of my grandmother's slippers against the plastic floor coaxed me awake. Around six o'clock my grandmother called us by our nicknames: "*J'mee! J'nell! Tong-boy! Kain na!* (Eat!)"

I rose slowly yet deliciously. My parents were already up and rushing to the hospital where they worked. They left without breakfast. When my siblings and I entered the kitchen, my grandmother kissed us on the cheeks. Her kisses were the special "Mama" kiss—she would bring my cheek near hers and inhale deeply.

Their constant movement took the place of verbal communication. While we ate, Mama slowly swept the already clean vinyl floors with a bamboo broom. My grandfather took out his cards and glasses and played solitaire on the table, which to me seemed little more than an endless shuffling of cards. I stood at his side, observing his preoccupation; he did not acknowledge me. But when I bent down to scratch my leg or retrieve a fallen card, he would turn his head, looking for me. Then he would return to the game.

Lunch was simple—a salty dried fish, *tuyo*, again accompanied by rice. My grandparents slowly picked out the bones, mixing the meat in the sticky rice with their fingers. In the afternoons, they sat together on the couch and watched their favorite soap operas, *Days of Our Lives* and *As the World Turns*. Occasionally, I sat on the floor near them and watched. Afterwards, my grandmother went into the garden and knelt by the flowers, while my grandfather busied himself in the garage, building small wooden benches for us. Then they softly ate dinner with my parents. Around nine p.m. they were in bed, awaiting the next quiet day.

II

I learned about the Bataan Death March from a couple of paragraphs pre-highlighted in used history books at school. Early in World War II, the Japanese forced thousands of Filipinos to march miles across their homeland. One such march was from Mariveles to San Fernando. There, the POWs were crammed into cargo trains, unloaded and forced to march again to Camp O'Donnell. If a prisoner collapsed, he was immediately shot or beaten to death. In the trains, there was no room for the dead to fall. Out of 70,000 prisoners—both Filipinos and American soldiers—only 45,000 reached the camp. After their arrival, at least 25,000 more Filipinos died within the first four months of captivity.

I was studying for a history test in high school and showed these small paragraphs to my father.

"Papa was in the Death March," my father said quietly.

He wouldn't say any more about my grandfather. I don't think he was trying to keep anything secret; it was simply the way the past existed in our family. Perhaps the idea of sharing emotions was distasteful to my father. Perhaps he wanted to protect me from the past. I wanted to learn the meaning of time. Perhaps he believed the world now has no need for the painful fragments of yesterday. I wanted to feel that pain. I needed to understand, to see, to learn. I wanted to know: Are Filipinos a little bit of every culture except ourselves, or do the pieces somehow form their own identity?

What I knew was that my grandparents had raised seven children on a sugar-cane farm. Mama held social dances and sewed beautiful dresses with puffy sleeves—*baro't saya*—for her daughters, debutantes of Luzon City. My grandfather was an engineer; he later taught military strategies at my father's school, which, as nepotism decreed, allowed my father to become the sergeant of his class. My grandparents made sure all of their children received a college education. Five went into the healthcare field, two became accountants.

But there was something I didn't know about their lives before these peaceful routines.

III

I am going halfway across the world to a place I have never been before. I am going home. My paternal grandfather—"Papa"—is the reason why I am going to the Philippines. He feels as though his time is near and wants his family, scattered throughout the United States, near him again.

When I arrive in Manila, there are at least twenty of my relatives waiting for me

JENNIFER F. ESTARIS

at the airport. They have brought me duty-free Toblerone, flowers, tropical fruits, a straw bag. They smile, laugh, hug, ask me about my flight, my family, my home. What is the *uso*—the trendy thing to do? Do you have any *tsismis* to tell us about your brother and sister, or those Hollywood celebrities? What is it like in your home, the States?

I smile and tell them that I am home now. They laugh, a happy, excited laugh—laughing because they are happy to see me, laughing because they want me to consider this country home, laughing because they like to laugh.

It is hot outside.

We travel in an air-conditioned van—a luxury—through the city, past brown people crossing the middle of the streets, jumping onto buses. Everywhere are jeepneys—remnants of World War II-surplus American G.I. jeeps repainted with flowering colors, folk art, silver lettering and now used as a mini mass transit system. We pass a marketplace, where rows of raw chickens sit out in the sun, flies swarming, people pointing at them with their pesos. Farther out, cement pipes awaiting construction sit atop one another, the holes covered by thin cloth. When we pause at a stoplight, I look closer. A cloth flutters from the opening of one of the pipes. A man comes out, goes to a neighboring tube and wakes up someone else. People live there. A few hours pass, and the scene changes from urban to rural poverty. Typhoons flooded the rice paddies, and the people are desolate, one distant relative tells me. I gaze across the hills overflowing with water. On the side of the road are two men, farmers perhaps, one holding a bamboo stick with string cast into the water, the other holding a sign telling motorists they have fresh fish for sale.

We continue on. I ask tentatively about my grandfather, hoping they won't think I am being too direct. They laugh. It seems that Filipinos are only indirect when in a foreign place. When they are home, everything is told. Loudly. With laughter. They say Papa is all right, he's been grumpy lately, he's stubborn, he's Papa. They say the stroke he suffered wasn't so bad; he can still talk, he gets lost in his words a few times, he needs to walk with a cane now, but mostly he's the same Papa. They laugh again, tumbling into the bright tones of Tagalog, pausing every now and then to translate if I look confused.

We arrive at the Rhodora compound—named in memory of my aunt. I settle in, trying to ignore the pervasive heat, and immediately everyone encourages me to eat: *Kain na!* Mama comes to me, slowly, with a smile on her face, trembling. She brings her face to my cheek and inhales.

We eat. *Adobong pusit. Sinigang. Pan de sal. Pinakbet. Ensaymada. Laing. Lumpia Shanghai. Siopao. Pancit luglug. Halo-halo.* Cute names, tasty dishes, different origins. But all definitely Filipino.

I fill my plate and sit to the side on a bamboo chair, observing the family—my family—interact. Then Papa arrives, late, waving everyone to continue eating, and comes toward me. I get up, place my dish to the side, and we share a brief hug before he waves me away.

"You eat," he says.

When the dishes are cleared, the relatives begin leaving, a kiss from each one. "We will pick you up tomorrow; we will go around the city; we will take you to this American restaurant called Friday's, it's the *uso, ba?*"

I nod, suppressing a giggle, and return to where my grandparents are sitting. "*J'mee...*" Mama motions for me to sit down on their plastic-covered couches. Her eyes are expectant; she wants to say more but cannot grasp the English. She has forgotten that I learned Tagalog by the sheer need to eavesdrop on my parents. Or perhaps she can no longer grasp Tagalog as well. My father's family speaks Pangasinan, a more gutteral, more percussive dialect with a different vocabulary and sentence structure altogether.

Papa watches me sit down, nods approvingly, and holds his cane with both of his hands, ready to rise. He remains.

"Your father said you want to know more about the family. About the past. About the war."

"Yes."

"I will tell you," he says.

His head lowers for a bit. Mama moves away from him to the other couch, still trembling, still looking at me with expectant eyes.

He begins his story, the words accented, disjointed. "During the war, this World

JENNIFER F. ESTARIS

War II, I was a medic. I was going to be an engineer and run our farm. But the war had started. The Americans had come, the Japanese had come, and the war had started, and I was to join the Allied Forces. I had just married Mama; we were just newly married."

Mama places her hands gently in her lap.

"I was not fighting; I wanted to help people. I did not know when I joined the army how horrible it would be. The pain. The wounds. The diseases. You could not help everyone, only just as much as you could. We were starving, there was so little food left. We ate horses, carabao, snakes, monkeys."

He brings his old hands to his forehead, squeezes. A faint sound comes from him.

"And Mama was at home, with our first born, your Tita Cleofe."

Mama stands up, shuffles over to a closet, brings out a bamboo broom and begins sweeping.

"The Japanese captured us; there was very little resistance. And once we were captured, they began to march us, in long lines, for many, many miles, shouting at us in Japanese, making us march without rest, without food, without water. We drank from puddles, which caused dysentery. So many men dying. Whenever someone fell down, they were kicked, shot, killed by bayonet, beheaded. They seemed to enjoy torturing us. One man found his father, who had fallen over, and was trying to help him up. He was trying to help him up, and—"

He stops again, holding his forehead.

"And he tried to explain that this was his father, and the enemy kept yelling at him. In the end, they killed his father. Right in front of him."

A long silence passes, broken only by the zip of Mama's slippers against the floor. Papa begins crying. I reach to get the box of tissues. In the meantime Mama has moved over to me, her hands signaling for me to give her the box. She nods her head, hands the tissues over to Papa. He looks at Mama's hands for a minute. She stands there next to him, silent. He dabs his eyes, clears his throat.

"I did not know anyone marching with me. We were all strangers, and we were all scared. I only thought of Mama, my family, my child. I knew that I would not survive. I was already sick. Only a matter of days before I, too, would collapse."

"We passed by rice fields. Endless rice paddies, hills, places to escape, places to run. I looked out over the land. I wanted to see Mama again. So I began to run. I've never ran faster in my life . . . I heard yelling from far away, commotion. I didn't turn back. Just running over the dryer footpaths of the fields. I saw little splashes of water around me. They were shooting. But I just ran."

By now, tears are streaming down his face, his body shaking. He cries for a while, Mama trying to hand him a new tissue. I rise, hold my grandfather.

I realize, in the hug, that the pieces I had been looking for all along were never really broken.

His tears stop, and he waves me away. His hands tighten over the knob of his cane, and he raises himself up.

"Mama," he calls, and she follows him.

The author with her father, in Saigon, 1968.   The author with her mother, in Saigon, 2000.

A RETURN TO VIETNAM

by Elsa Arnett

It is early evening when the taxi inches into the narrow alley. Halfway down, I ask the driver to pull over. I need to take the last steps at my own pace.

A faint drizzle falls as I fix my eyes on the end of the road. As I adjust to the darkness, I can see the house, about thirty steps away, at the curve of the cul-de-sac. The last time I was on this road, I was four. That was thirty years ago. I was born here in Saigon, Vietnam, and raised at this very place. I can make out the iron gate. The leafy *vu sua* tree dotted with milky fruit. And the outlines of the modest colonial villa—my childhood house.

Right away, I know. I should never have come back.

My family left Vietnam in 1971, when we moved to the United States. I had not returned since. In part, this was because the communist government for decades restricted travel to Vietnam. But mostly it was because I did not want to. But about a month ago, my editor asked me to go on a two-month reporting assignment to Vietnam. To him, it must have seemed like a natural fit. My father, Peter Arnett, spent thirteen years as a Western journalist chronicling the American military's ill-fated effort in Vietnam. My Vietnamese mother, along with half of her family, fled the communists from the north to the south and, eventually, to the United States. I am also fluent in Vietnamese. And on top of that, I had just written a dozen articles for a special section on the twenty-fifth anniversary of the fall of Saigon.

I was in the unusual position of having lived through the Vietnam War as a child, yet also of having the distance to dissect that turbulent time as a detached American journalist. But what my editor didn't know was that Vietnam was not only a place and a war, but also a large part of my personal history that I have long tried to bury. For years, I didn't have any Vietnamese friends, I didn't eat at Vietnamese restaurants, I didn't watch Vietnam War movies, and I didn't read a single one of my father's prize-winning dispatches. What I hadn't realized, and what I would only come to understand during the emotionally grueling weeks in Vietnam, was why I felt such hostility toward a place I could barely remember.

—⚡—

It is wedged in the corner of my mother's closet, midway in a wobbly stack of family photo albums. It is a felt-covered scrapbook in powder blue, with bright yellow ducklings marching across the front: my baby album. In one black-and-white photo, I am in the protective grip of my father's arms, my head bare as a grapefruit. In another, I am about to blow out the two candles on my birthday cake. When I look at these photos, I can recall the sensation of squirming out of my grandmother's lap as she tries to spoon-feed me chicken porridge. And I remember wrapping my little hand around my grandfather's pinkie as we wander in our garden, plucking yellow chrysan-themums to put on the altar for his daily prayer.

The good memories I have of Vietnam end there, around the time I left Vietnam for the United States. The remaining memories are different, seared into my mind over the three decades since. I remember seeing my mother in our New York living room, crying, lighting slender sticks of incense on every anniversary of her brother's death. She was a schoolgirl when she last saw him. They were separated by the division of Vietnam in 1954. Decades later, she learned he was dead. I remember hearing about my grandparents fleeing a crumbling Saigon, leaving behind their house and their identities. They showed up on my family's doorstep in America in dark overcoats three sizes too big, their possessions reduced to what they could jam into a blue British Airways shoulder bag. And I remember watching my aunt twist off the head of my favorite doll—the one with the auburn curls—so she could smuggle three tightly rolled $100 bills to my relatives trapped in Vietnam.

At times, I try to convince myself the pain is all in the past. But once, when my mother and I visited the Bay Area and went into the surrounding hills, where I felt tranquility, she felt something else: panic, fear and dread. She told me the mountains reminded her of the weeks she spent as a child scrambling for safety in the snarled jungles of North Vietnam. She had shivered under piles of leaves, delirious with malaria. Thorny branches scratched her limbs. She ate only potatoes and wild roots. Sometimes, I won't think about the bad memories for months. Other times, such as when I am buckled in a plane for my two-day flight to Vietnam, they come rushing forth. I shift uncomfortably in my narrow seat. I flip through a guidebook. It opens to a map of Vietnam. I see the names of places I heard about long ago: Vinh An and Hanoi—places in the North from where my mother fled. Then I see Da Nang and Ben Tre—sites of fierce battles my father covered in the South. It starts to become clear. My journey will be as much about reconciling the Vietnam in my mind as it will be about coming to terms with the Vietnam before my eyes.

—⁓—

At daybreak, the pilot announced we were on approach to Hanoi. Lush patches of green fields, some a pale celadon, others a deep moss, stretched to the horizon. Dozens of small waterways wove in and out of the terrain like threads. With the airplane engine buzzing in my ear, my first thought was that this must have been the same view seen by American bombers.

When I stepped off the plane, I saw a silent ceremony taking place on the tarmac several hundred feet away. Right away I realized that even though a quarter-century may have passed, the legacy of the war continued. Lined up in two rows behind a gray U.S. Air Force cargo plane were nearly a dozen metal containers. Caskets. Inside were the remains of American servicemen who had been missing in action. I was jarred by the sight. In the breezeless, dreary morning, it looked almost like something from a grainy, black-and-white newsreel. But it was happening right then. Seeing the stark caskets, I was overcome by sadness. And guilt.

ELSA ARNETT

I know these soldiers had been sent to fight by the U.S. government. And I know that the reasons the American government wanted to win the war in Vietnam had more to do with containing communism than with protecting the welfare of families like mine. But I also know American soldiers were a beacon of hope for millions of Vietnamese who could not imagine life under communism. And in the end, regardless, they did die for families like mine.

And even made my life possible. My father was a young newspaper reporter from New Zealand en route by ship to the newspapers in London's Fleet Street in the late 1950s. Along his journey, he made stops to cover insurrections and civil unrests in Laos, Indonesia and Thailand. The intensifying American military conflict in Vietnam held his interest. So did a Vietnamese woman he met at a cocktail party whose glossy black hair glimmered under the hazy moonlight—my mother. By the time I was born, the war was well under way. I was four months old when communist troops blasted their way into Saigon during the Lunar New Year celebrations in what became known as the Tet Offensive. My family had been asleep for barely an hour when several deafening bangs awoke them. My mother thought they were New Year firecrackers. My father knew better. He bundled me up in a mattress and wedged it in the bathtub. Then he went into the streets to cover the fighting, while my mother hovered over me.

At that point, there were nearly 500,000 U.S. soldiers in Vietnam. Public approval of President Johnson's handling of the war slipped to 26 percent. Anti-war protesters in the United States began to flood the streets. It would be years before I would have any idea what these events would mean to the global balance of power, to the American psyche, to my family's lives and to me.

—⟶✺⟵—

Though I spent most of my life in the United States, bits of Vietnamese culture seeped into my American childhood. I spoke to my mother in Vietnamese. As my schoolmates ate bologna sandwiches for lunch, I ate sticky rice and shredded dried pork. Before I got on airplanes, my mother would press her palms together in front of an ivory Buddha to pray for a safe journey. Beyond that, I felt little connection to my birthplace.

Growing up, I cringed when I heard melodramatic Vietnamese pop music. And I retreated to my room when my mother invited her Vietnamese friends over for dinner. Will plunging myself into Vietnam feel familiar or foreign? The answer comes with rapid force. First, the heat: stifling, unrelenting. I perspire through my shirt in four minutes. Then, the images along the bumpy highway from the airport to downtown Hanoi: villagers in conical hats bent over tender shoots of rice; children perched atop water buffalo; a cluster of schoolgirls pedaling on their bicycles, the tails of their creamy *ao dai* dresses fluttering behind them. Then, the chaos of the city: the chatter of Vietnamese voices at the congested outdoor markets; the fragrance of anise from a noodle soup stall; thatched baskets filled with juicy, fist-sized green fruit that resemble grenades. And at every corner, the ubiquitous cyclos—armies of pedicabs.

I understood what people were saying. I recognized the exotic fruits. I had experienced all this before. The memories came back, bit by bit. I was comforted. Down the block, I saw a man balancing a wooden pole with a metal canister hanging from each end. I chased him. I asked him to open the lid. Can it be? Inside the vat was a gleaming, smooth, pearly custard made of tofu. This ginger-laced dessert was my childhood favorite. I had thought about it hundreds of times. I had eaten it in the United States, but it had never tasted as good. Finally, I was to have it again. The man ladled a generous serving into a bowl, puzzled by my excitement. I cradled the bowl in my palms and took a big gulp. But something wasn't right. It was lukewarm, thin, almost tasteless. Too little sugar? Too much water? All I knew was that it didn't measure up to my expectation.

The tofu teaches me a lesson. This place feels like home, but it isn't. This Vietnam is a different place and a different time. And I am a different person. My clothes, my accent, my purchasing power and my tangled memories set me apart from the country I am standing in. My roots may be here, but they were buried long ago.

—⁂—

I was bracing for the moment I was to go to my eldest aunt's house in Hanoi. There, I was to meet relatives whom I had never seen before. Although we were bound by blood, we had been separated by invisible barriers of culture and politics,

ELSA ARNETT

and connected only in fragments. My cousin, for example, was named after me because her parents hoped she would have a life like mine. I had wondered about my relatives left behind in Vietnam. The only picture I had seen of them together was taken when my mother was an impish-looking youngster. They had been like characters in a novel—rich in my imagination, absent in my life.

I could always tell when my mother received a letter from relatives in Vietnam. There was a flutter of excitement, followed by silence as she read and re-read the contents, followed by despair when she digested what it said. These letters never came through the mail. While I was growing up, people in Vietnam were forbidden to communicate with the United States. So the letters had to be smuggled. Sometimes they were delivered by a friend of a friend who worked in a foreign embassy. Other times by my father passing through on a reporting assignment. The letters were sporadic. In a good year, my mother might get one. I remember trying to stop her crying. But she was years away, somewhere in the chaos of the final days before she left Hanoi in 1955, frantically getting her transit papers in order before heading south.

At my aunt's house in Hanoi, we were all reunited. My mother and two aunts, who flew in from the United States, introduced me to the crowd. Everyone was assembled: aunts, uncles, cousins, nieces, nephews. We all embraced. My relatives giggled as I spoke Vietnamese, and they searched my face for familiar features. Then I met my eldest aunt. She was a tiny, elegant figure, wearing a pale silk blouse with a strand of pearls, her silvery hair pulled back in a perfect bun. While the rest of us were sweltering, she looked remarkably comfortable. She moved with unhurried gestures like someone from another time, and she spoke with a gentle voice, though I was told she could be stern. I saw in her face the same expression of tenderness that I saw in my grandparents as they waited at my elementary school each afternoon to pick me up.

I bent over to wrap my arms around her. I felt like I was eight, hugging my grandparents again. My aunt was in her seventies, the same age as my grandparents when they came to America. When they died years later, I felt I had lost forever the connection to two special people who lived through decades of bloodshed and deprivation and found the determination to survive. My grandparents had a quiet dignity and strength. And I saw it again, for the first time, in my aunt. I spent balmy evenings on her couch in the living room, my arms intertwined in hers, my head slumped on her shoulder. She fretted over whether I was eating enough or whether I was working too hard, just as my grandparents did. It was reassuring. After only a few days, I felt as though I had known her all my life. And in a way, I had.

In my uncle I saw traces of other relatives: my mother's almond-shaped eyes, my aunt's coarse, black hair, my grandfather's wiry build. My uncle was the only one of my mother's three brothers who had survived, and through him I got a glimpse of what life may have been like before the war, when he was just a school kid, talking, joking, teasing. He still called my two aunts by childhood nicknames. They reminisced about long-ago crushes. They drove by their old schools. They visited old friends. Often, it seemed as if they were picking up conversations that had ended in mid-sentence more than forty years ago. There was much to catch up on. And they all seemed desperate to make up for lost time. Occasionally, the conversations became strained. They bickered over things that happened more than a quarter-century ago. Was it right, my uncle asked repeatedly, to take my grandparents to the United States during the fall of Saigon? To displace them from the only country they had ever known? To separate them forever from half their children and grandchildren? My mother and aunts became defensive. Voices rose. Opinions held firm.

Time had moved on for my family in the United States as they adjusted to a new life in a new country. But in Vietnam, resentments remained. My uncle didn't like to talk about the decades of suffering during, and especially immediately after, the war. But I pressed him. He told me many people lived like animals. I pressed him more. He told me that for years, he, his wife and two young daughters lived on several ounces of beef, a few cups of rice and drops of cooking oil a month. Neither one of us said anything for a while. Then, he asked, "Elsa, you've never had to suffer in your life, have you?"

I had suffered in various ways at school, at work, in life. But I knew what he meant. He meant suffering for survival. And, no, I never had. It was hard for me to imagine. Then I realized that, perhaps more than anything, I will always be an outsider

ELSA ARNETT

in Vietnam because there are fundamental experiences that so many people here share, which I cannot comprehend.

—⁓—

It is the first address I ever memorized: 36 Tran Cao Van. My childhood home. My family's old house in downtown Ho Chi Minh City is on a quiet cul-de-sac off a busy commercial street in what was then an affluent Saigon neighborhood, a few blocks from the former U.S. Embassy. Most of my life in Vietnam was spent at this house, a sprawling single-story colonial with a courtyard and gardens. It was in this house that I fell asleep in my grandfather's arms in a cocoon of gauzy white mosquito netting. That I played with blocks on the black-and-white tile floor of the dining room while my family feasted on roasted squab. I remember our gentle brown mutt named Lucky, and my doomed attempts to raise four fuzzy chicks, all devoured by rats the first evening I got them.

When I had first considered returning to Vietnam, I knew I would have to visit my old house. But I was apprehensive. Did I want to risk tainting those idyllic memories? My house was sure to have deteriorated. But I had been entirely unprepared for the degree to which things had changed. And even now, I was unprepared for how much it would hurt to see the changes. I put off visiting my childhood house for as long as I could. I claimed I was too busy working, or that it was raining too hard. But finally, with just a few days left in Vietnam, I decided to face my fear. My mother, two aunts and I squeezed into a taxi. I get restless. I keep asking, "Are we there yet?" Eventually, the driver turns into the cul-de-sac. He pulls over so I can walk the final steps. It is getting dark, and it has begun to rain, so it is hard to see the outlines of anything. I sense that the alley is narrower than I remember.

I notice that what used to be my neighbors's leafy courtyards had been paved over, that the open space was converted to rooms, many of which came right up to the street. Some homes have been turned into bars, with neon signs and the stench of stale beer. Already, it's clear this was not a good idea. Then I look to the end of the cul-de-sac. I can see my family's old gate. I step into the courtyard. I have to blink several times to make sure I am seeing what I think I am seeing. What is left of my family home is in ruins. Where my one extended family had lived, now six families are crammed together. The white gate once adorned with lush branches of pink bougainvillea is rusted and bare. The patio where I had perched on a rattan chair to blow out birthday candles is unrecognizable. In its place are stacks of dirty bowls and cooking pots, tin cans, egg shells and mango peels. Large swaths of our garden had been covered in concrete. The rooms of the house have been subdivided with crude walls, turning the once-attractive private residence into a maze of apartments. I wander through our old house as though in a nightmare. An aunt takes my arm and leads me through the rooms, the current tenants indifferent to our presence. "Was this our living room?" I ask incredulously, as I stare at a run-down space that has been converted into a public bar. "Yes," she answers. As she motions me into different parts of the house, we both begin to cry. Outside, my mother and another aunt stand near the gate. They had taken this tour before. They weren't going to put themselves through it again.

I strain to try to place some of my good memories in this squalor. But all that comes to me are the thoughts that I usually block out. I remember my aunt recounting how just days before they fled Saigon, they gathered around a bonfire in the court-yard, tossing in armfuls of photographs, journals my grandmother kept and precious letters from relatives in the north. I remember my grandmother telling me how she left the house in such despair on that final day in April 1975 that she couldn't bear to turn back and look at it one last time. I remember that my aunt and uncle from Hanoi had made a trip to our house several months after Saigon fell. At that time, the communists had not yet seized the house. My grandfather's collection of French history books were still on the shelves. My father's white Karmann Ghia was still in the driveway. It was as though my family had merely stepped out for the afternoon. I am getting dizzy—the humidity, the rain, these thoughts. I motion to my aunt that I have had enough. I want to leave. My mind is trying to make sense of everything I see. My heart is aching in disappointment. Like my grandmother, I don't look back.

—〜—

ELSA ARNETT

There is a Vietnamese folk song called "Mother's Legacy" that I heard so often when growing up in Vietnam, I know it by heart. It goes something like this:

A thousand years colonized by the Chinese,
A hundred years colonized by the French,
Twenty years, each day, a civil war.
Mother's legacy for her children,
Mother's legacy is this sad Viet country.

My mother tried very hard to shield me from her suffering. She sacrificed so I would never have to endure what she had to. She rarely talked about the hardships in her life. When I pressed her for details, she changed the subject or offered vague answers. But she didn't realize that her silence was even more revealing. She didn't realize that when her eyes clouded over and her face fell into a frown, she passed on to me the melancholy of Vietnam the same way she passed on her straight, dark hair and chestnut-colored eyes. Eventually, her resentments became mine. Then I added my own confusions, my own interpretations, until I decided years ago that I wanted to avoid anything associated with Vietnam. That way, I could somehow outmaneuver my feelings. But demonizing Vietnam only intensified the hurt.

Going back forced me to confront my jumble of emotions. I discovered that some of my fears were justified, some exaggerated. I realized there are things that will always make me angry, but there are things I could let go. It is too late for my mother to erase the bitterness over the decades of separation from her relatives. But perhaps it isn't too late for me. I know there is no way to obliterate my painful memories. However, there is plenty of time to make new memories.

The day I leave is a muggy, overcast morning, and I am late for the airport. I first have to go to my eldest aunt's house in Hanoi to say good-bye. When I get there, everyone is assembled, just as they were the first day I saw them. This time, their faces aren't animated with anticipation but glum with the prospect of farewells. I embrace each person. My namesake cousin clings to my waist. My uncle, who shuns public displays of affection, obliges with a hug. My nieces and nephews, always noisy and rambunctious, are subdued. Then, I get to my aunt, who is usually composed and dignified. Only now, her face is anguished. Her arms are outstretched. It breaks my heart. I don't know how long I hold her, but it isn't enough. It has taken me more than thirty years to meet her, and she is frail and has a heart condition. I don't know when, or if, I will see her again. Reluctantly, I pry my arms from her and step into the taxi. The car begins to pull away. My family stands on the curb, waving and weeping. And this time, I look back.

ELSA ARNETT

Walter Lee, on the bridge of the *MS American Leader.*

AN OFFICER AND A CHINAMAN:
A WAR HERO I NEVER MET

by Christopher Lee

PROLOGUE

When I was maybe six or seven years old, my mother told me that I had an uncle who had died in World War II. He was "the first Chinese Officer in the Merchant Marine." It was an intriguing statement. I could tell that it held pride for her and for Chinese people. From then on, whenever I heard his name, it was accompanied by "he was the first Chinese Officer in the Merchant Marine." Here was a role model for me. We lived in a California suburb in the 1950s and there were no Asians on TV, in magazines, or in advertisements. Certainly there were no Chinese cowboys, super-heroes, or actors. I wanted to know more about this uncle, and I wanted him to be a role model, but there was little my mother could tell me.

Many years later, I began a serious search, but found out very little. While I had heard of this Uncle Walter many times, the lack of tangible evidence of his life made it hard to believe that he really existed. I posed questions to relatives, possible acquaintances, and of course my mother. Little surfaced. I regreted never meeting him. Once, while in the kitchen with my Uncle George and my mother (Walter's brother and sister), I asked "When was Walter's birthday?" They looked at each other, something passed between them, then they both shook their heads and said they didn't know. "We didn't celebrate birthdays. Well, not officially. Sometimes, if we came home and there was chicken for dinner, it *might* mean it was someone's birthday." It was hard to believe. Getting information was far more difficult than I thought it would be. And there was a blankness from both of them, a stone-walling of sorts. Intuitively, not consciously, I recognized Uncle Walter's story as "one of those things we don't talk about." Later, I realized that it was because it was a story with a sad and abrupt end. It was about someone they loved dearly, a brother who had a bright future, great hopes, and great dreams…and then his life ended tragically.

THE MEDAL / THE POSTCARDS

My mother gave me Walter's Mariner's Medal when I was about fifteen. It had been presented posthumously to "Goongsie," my grandfather. I was quite impressed. It was a heavy, solid, real thing connected to the man. It wasn't like cheesy medals and awards I'd seen before. This was the real thing. For decades I kept it, getting it out once in a while and looking at it. Its solemn solidity somehow made real the fact of Walter's life and honor.

A few years ago, I received a little packet of old postcards from Walter's World War II voyages (found by my mother while cleaning). These almost substantiated the fact that he once lived. I could see his actual handwriting and signature. There was a postmark and a date, even some marks from U.S. censors. Here were things he had touched and signed. Before seeing these physical, tangible objects, Walter was as illusory to me as a story in a history book or a picture in a newspaper. The medal and the postcards gave me a few clues, but I still had no idea what the Merchant Marine was, where to look for more information, or how to begin.

SOURCES

I visited the library at the Coast Guard Academy in Vallejo and got some tiny bits of information. A letter accompanying the Mariner's Medal stated that Walter's vessel was the *MS American Leader.* I looked up the ship at the Academy's library and found the following account:

> *The merchant ship* American Leader *was built in 1941 at San Francisco (Western Pipe and Steel in Richmond, CA) and delivered to the American Pioneer Line*

division of the United States Lines. It was attacked and sunk by the German raider Michel on September 10, 1942. The ship was en route from Colombo, Ceylon, to Newport News, Virginia, via Cape Town, South Africa. [Walter was the ship's pilot! He was listed as a lieutenant.]

The American Leader had left Cape Town on September 7, 1942 and was carrying a cargo of rubber, coconut oil, copra, liquid latex, opium, tobacco, rugs, and other general cargo. At the time of the attack, she was about 800 miles west of the

MS American Leader

Company: United States Lines. New York, NY
Master: Haakon A. Pederson
Built: 1941 @ San Francisco, CA
Dimensions: 397' x 60' x 26'

Fig. 1 — The *MS American Leader*.

Cape of Good Hope. She had forty-nine merchant crew and nine Naval Armed Guards. Ten of the crew were killed during the attack. The remainder of the crew were taken prisoner aboard the raider.[1]

The raider Michel appeared off the starboard bow of the American Leader about 1930 ship time and opened fire with her deck guns. The shells smashed the #1 lifeboat and damaged a life raft. The radio equipment was destroyed and kerosene drums on deck were hit and burst into flames. While the crew was trying to launch the #2 lifeboat, shells struck the davits (small cranes used to lift the lifeboat), putting that boat out of commission. The ship was then struck by two torpedoes. She settled by the stern and sank in about twenty-five minutes. The survivors clustered together on rafts and were picked up by the raider about six hours after the ship had sunk.

---

[1] Shortly after I completed this work, I met Captain George Duffy through the web. He was a shipmate of Walter's, the junior 3rd officer on the *American Leader*. Walter was his mentor. He said that there were 47 survivors, 11 lost. The raider picked up the survivors, transferred them to the *Uckermark* on October 7. From there, they were taken to Batavia, Java and handed over to the Japanese on November 6. According to Captain Duffy, Walter was on the bridge when the attack occurred, and so was a natural target for the raider. His knee or leg was injured in that first attack and never healed properly. He had a limp in the prison camp.

CHRISTOPHER LEE

Those accounts gave me a good picture of the event that led to Walter's eventual death. I felt my heartbeat increase and my imagination race as I read the account of the attack on the ship. Fire! Hot lead whistling across the deck! A smashed brig, men scurrying to launch lifeboats, another attack and the destruction of the lifeboat, a fast sinking of the *American Leader*, and then men on rafts as the ship sank and the German raider closed in. And six hours later they were picked up out of the water? If they were hit at 1930 ship's time, that meant it was after midnight before they were rescued!

Also, from the same Library, I found out about the Mariner's Medal:

The Mariner's Medal was established on May 10, 1943, for any seaman who, while serving on a ship of the Merchant Service, is wounded, undergoes physical injury, or suffers through dangerous exposure as a result of an act of the enemy of the United States.

Fig. 2 — Front and Back of the Mariner's Medal, awarded posthumously to Goongsie in memory of Walter.

I wrote to sources suggested by the Coast Guard Librarian. From the U.S. Coast Guard, a Marine Personnel Documentation Specialist sent me Walter's service record. He was listed as Mr. Walter H. Lee, Z-15673, deceased. Some very interesting "Certificates of Discharge" were included. These records showed the length of a voyage, the ship, his rank at the time, the place of shipment and the place of discharge. I found later that the Certificates were put in service records only if the shipping companies that employed the vessel sent them to the Department of Transportation. Prior to World War II, few of these records appeared in the file.

The Department of Transportation directed me to write to the Director of the National Maritime Center for the U.S. Coast Guard. From them, I received a wealth of information: certificates, 3rd Mate's License, and more! Actual documents were sent! Proof of his existence! Even a picture of him from one of his license applications! Finally, my sister gave me a photo album that belonged to Walter's brother, our Uncle George. Within those photos were a few, scant pictures of Walter.

From all this I sewed together the following story of Walter's life, an Officer and a Chinaman.

THE STORY

Walter Hay Lee was born on August 23, 1913. He was the third child of the family. Marian and George were the elders, and my mother, Edna, was the baby. The family lived at 802 North Alameda Street, Los Angeles, California in the old Chinatown. (That Chinatown is no longer there. The entire neighborhood was torn down in the 1930s and the family moved to 743 East 27th Street, Los Angeles.) My mother said that the name of a German midwife, Anna Mueller, is on her birth certificate, and "In all probability, she [Mrs. Mueller] delivered George and Walter, too." That seems likely. Mrs. Mueller delivered most of the children of Los Angeles's Chinatown during that era. Lisa See's wonderful book *On Gold Mountain* talks about this. The neighborhood she describes is also Walter's. His house was directly behind the See's compound, on Alameda Street.

Fig. 3 — Earliest known photo of Walter (1929?), on a Los Angeles Chinatown playground with a football.

Those who knew Walter recall a boy with a cheerful, active and vigorous personality. He was friendly, easy to talk to, and outgoing. Around 1919, Goongsie took George, Walter, and Edna to China. They went to the village of Marian's fiancee to meet the family of the prospective groom. According to the stories, Walter was the outgoing son. He'd walk up to people, greet them, visit, and talk. George and Edna hung back and weren't as forthcoming.

Both Walter and George played musical instruments through their high school years. George played the trombone, and Walter played either the tuba or the baritone. Edna remembers seeing the instrument. The picture below shows Walter with such a horn.

Fig. 4 — Native Sons of the Golden State (N.S.G.S.). Walter is tallest in the back row, sixth from the left.

Uncle George said that they kept their instruments in a shed in the alley behind their house. One day, when they went out there, they found that someone had broken into it. Among other things, their instruments had been stolen.

The brothers were also active in baseball, basketball, and tennis. They played on the local basketball team together and both of them were six feet tall, which was quite tall for Chinese people of the time and place. Most Chinese in the United States before 1980 were from the Guandong province and not very tall. Notes and pictures from George's scrapbook state that the average height of "the Squad" was 5'11"! They called themselves L.O.W.A.: "League of Western Athletes."

While Marian went to Lincoln High School and George and Edna went to Jefferson High School, Walter went to Polytechnic High. He majored in Engineering at Polytechnic and joined the Merchant Marine in 1933 shortly before graduating.

Figs. 5, 6 — Left, Walter playing Chinatown Basketball, c. 1932, and above, the L.O.W.A. Squad. Walter is third from the left.

He was a dispatch clerk in San Pedro and studied navigation while attending a San Francisco Naval school.

Edna believes that Goongsie got Walter into the Merchant Marine through connections. Goongsie was the agent for the Dollar Steamship Line and knew about the Merchant Marine, the Academies, and who to see. Training for officers before the war was a one-year program.

Walter obtained his "Record of Certificate of Efficiency to Lifeboat Man" from the Port of Los Angeles, Base 17, U.S. Coast Guard, on March 7th, 1934, roughly six months into his "training." His "Certificate of Service to Able Seaman" certifies that on the fourteenth day of September, 1934, Walter H. Lee was twenty-one years of age. He was rated as an Able Seaman for service on the "high seas and any inland waters [and] was rated able seaman upon examination as to his knowledge of the duties of seamanship." Again, this came from the Port of Los Angeles, roughly one year into his training, and certifies the "365 days" at sea described by veteran merchant mariners as the requirement of an A.B.S.

Walter's Third Mate papers were issued on April 6, 1937, so it appears that the young seaman spent a year at sea and in classes before getting his A.B.S., then spent another two years learning mathematics, ship construction, Admiralty Law, stability, stowage, ship handling, and everything else the Coast Guard would throw at him before he took his exams for Junior Third Officer.

But what was Walter like in these days? Edna recalls that when Walter came home on leave, he would use a car for a date and to go out with his friends. He and George shared a car, but George was always more "relaxed" about upkeep. Edna remembers Walter muttering and fuming: "That George! All he does is *drive* the car. He never washes it or cleans it. He just doesn't take *care* of things!" And he'd get a bucket of water, go out and wash the car with spit, polish and vigor. Whether it was life at sea or just the difference in the brother's personalities is hard to say. Probably both.

Maryan Gong, the niece of Walter, lived for a short while with her family in the Lee home in Los Angeles. She recalls how when she was a young girl of five or six, Walter came home and carried her on is shoulders, being *big* and *strong* and vigorous. She thought he was a lot of fun.

Edna also recalls that Walter had to be pretty tough and ready. She said that once in a while a sailor would get rebellious and refuse to do duty or follow a command, and Walter sometimes had to knock the man down, just to keep order.

A 1937 document from the Port of Los Angeles lists him as six feet tall with brown eyes, black hair, and a "medium" complexion (!). While this is the only reference to Walter's racial features, research reveals that the pre-WWII Merchant Marine was composed of an international body of sailors from all walks of life. On any given ship, there would be Scandanavians, Germans, Americans, Greeks, and others. Into this mix walked Walter, the first Chinese Officer, although there were probably other Asian seamen.

This photograph was affixed to Walter's April 6, 1937, 3rd Mate's License. If it is a 1937 photo, it would make him almost twenty-four years old.

PHOTOGRAPH

Applicant to affix his signature

VOYAGES

Walter must have made training voyages and voyages as a navigator and seaman. No "discharge papers" for those have been found. Between his graduation from Polytechnic in 1933 and his first documented voyage in 1940, Walter must have made at least six to ten voyages, maybe as many as twice those numbers.

Below is a list of the voyages he is known to have made as an officer:

Sea Witch	July 30, 1940 out of Tampa, Florida	Jr. 3rd Officer
Sea Witch	Aug. 20, 1940 out of New York	Jr. 3rd Officer
Sea Witch	Jan 10, 1941 out of New York	3rd Officer
Sea Witch	April 19, 1941 out of New York	3rd Officer
MS American Leader	June 17, 1941 out of San Francisco	3rd Officer
MS American Leader	October 18, 1941 out of New York	2nd Officer
MS American Leader	April 13, 1942 out of New York	2nd Officer

Edna says that Walter's ship was in Manila when Pearl Harbor was attacked, December 7, 1941, probably on his second cruise with the *American Leader*. The dates correspond. Walter told her that there were special procedures to follow if Japan attacked Pearl Harbor while the Merchant Marines were in Manila: the captain of the ship was to open the safe and follow the orders placed there in a sealed envelope. Walter said that the captain opened the safe and found that the ship was silently to pull up anchor, drift away, and not start up her engines until they were five miles out to sea. They escaped at that time, but must have returned.

Manila was attacked by the Japanese on January 2, 1942, only twenty-seven days later. Manila surrendered on February 24, 1942. The dates of the discharges show that Walter was on the *American Leader* at that time. It appears that it made it back to New York safely, only to go out again in April on its last trip.

On his final voyage, Walter was one of the pilots. Mom said that he was coming home to take the next level of exams, which would be for first officer. Those who became first officers became captains of their own ships. Walter had never failed his exams. He would have been the first Asian ship's captain in the Merchant Marine. It was never to happen.

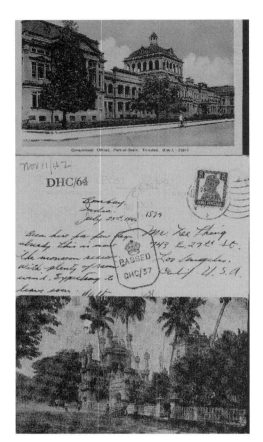

Fig. 7 — Postcards from Walter's last voyage.

The four postcards I have were all sent during his last voyage. They are intriguing, brief, and exotic in their own ways. Walter couldn't say much except to comment on the weather, since it was wartime and letters and postcards fell under the scrutiny of the U.S. censors. The cards from San Fernando, Trinidad, Port of Spain, Cape Town, South Africa, somewhere in India [This postcard is stamped with a U.S. Censorship Examination mark], and from Colombo, Ceylon.

WALTER'S LAST VOYAGE

From this point on, the story becomes one of telegrams, secrecy, and mystery. Walter's ship, the *American Leader*, was sunk on September 7, 1942, en route from Ceylon to Newport News, Virginia. Telegrams were sent to his father (erroneously referred to as Mr. Leo Lee several times)

> November 5, 1942: The Navy Department deeply regrets to inform you that your son, Walter H. Lee is missing following action in the performance of his duty and in the service of his country. The coast guard appreciates your great anxiety and will furnish you further information promptly when received. To prevent possible aid to our enemies, please do not divulge the name of his ship.
> — Vice Admiral R.R. Waesche commandant U.S. Coast Guard

May 12, 1943: The Provost Marshal General directs me to transmit to you the following short wave radio message from Walter Hay Lee, Seaman, which originated in Japan:

> I AM NOW PRISONER OF WAR IN JAVA. MOST OF THE CREW ARE
> SAFE. GET IN TOUCH WITH U.S. LINES FOR INSURANCE MONEY
> AND WAGES DUE TO ME. ALSO WRITE TO SEAMANS SAVING BANK,
> WALL STREET, NEW YORK, FOR MY SAVINGS. I AM FINE AND AM
> HOPING THAT THIS WAR WILL END SOON, SO I'LL BE FREE AGAIN.
> WITH BEST REGARDS AND LOVE TO MOTHER AND OTHERS.

The War Department is unable to verify this message. You may communicate with Mr. Lee by following the inclosed [sic] directions for sending ordinary mail. If further information from any source is received by this office in regard to Walter Hay Lee, you will be advised at once.

Sincerely yours,

Howard F. Bresee, Colonel, C.M.P., Chief, Information Bureau

Quite sadly, Walter's shortwave message bears evidence to the isolation of the prisoners. Walter did not know that his mother had died in August of 1942.

June 8, 1943   CONFIDENTIAL

Dear Mr. Lee:

With further reference to our telegram of 5 November, 1942 reporting your son as missing, you are advised that we are now in receipt of an official report from the Prisoner of War Information Bureau, through the International Red Cross, that Walter Hay Lee is a prisoner of war of Japan. He is interned in the Prisoner of War Camp, Java. The enclosed directions will enable you to send your son any ordinary mail. The United States Coast Guard wishes to express its appreciation of your patient forbearance in the face of such deep anxiety. By direction of the Commandant.

Very truly yours,

R.H. Faringholt, Lieutenant (T), USCGR, Chief,

Merchant Marine Personnel, Records and Welfare Section

June 21, 1943

Dear Mr. Lee:

The Provost marshal General directs me to forward to you the inclosed short wave radio message which was intercepted by government facilities.

The War Department is unable to verify this message and it is not to be construed as an official notification. If additional information concerning the above named person is received from any source, you will be advised.

> Sincerely yours,
>
> Howard F. Bresee, Colonel, C.M.P., Chief, Information Bureau

September 5, 1945

Dear Mr. Lee:

With reference to our letter of 5 June, 1945, advising you that your son, Walter Hay Lee, was reported interned in the Java prisoner of war camp.

It is with deep regret that we must now inform you that a report has been received by the Prisoner of War Information Bureau listing your son as missing, following the sinking of a Japanese transport which was transporting prisoners from the Java Camp to the Malay Camp on 18 September, 1944. The Coast Guard appreciates your great anxiety in receiving this information and you may be assured that if any further information concerning your son is received, you will be promptly notified. By direction of the Commandant.

> Very truly yours,
>
> R.H. Farinholt, Lt. Cmdr., USCGN(T), Chief,
>
> Merchant Marine Personnel, Records and Welfare Section

Goongsie replied on September 21, 1945. In beautiful handwriting, he bemoans the fact that the above letter informed him of Walter's M.I.A. status a year after the event! He asks how many prisoners were on board the ship and how many were saved.

September 27, 1945

The only information received concerning this casualty is a cable from Tokyo received by the Prisoner of War Information Bureau on 1, September, 1945, and headed:

TOKYO CABLES FOLLOWING PSON MISSING DURING TRANSPORT FROM JAVA CAMP TO MALAY CAMP WHEN SHIP SUNK BY ENEMY SUBMARINE ON SEPTEMBER EIGHTEENTH 1944 OFF EAST COAST SUMATRA.

Below this heading there are listed eight names, one of which is your son's name. No information concerning the number of prisoners on board the transport, the number of casualties, or the number or names of survivors is given. You were advised of the casualty as soon as the cable was received by this office.

November 29, 1945
Mr. Erich Nielsen, Secretary
Maritime War Emergency Board
War Shipping Administration
Department of Commerce Building
Washington 25, D.C.
The attached letter of 19 November, 1945, requesting that a certificate of death in the case of Walter Hay Lee be mailed to the Group Death Claim Division, Metropolitan Life Insurance Company, 1 Madison Avenue, New York, New York, is forwarded as a matter coming under your jurisdiction. The writer has not been informed of this reference. By direction of the Commandant.
R.H. Farinholt, Lt. Comdr., USCGR (T), Chief,
Merchant Marine Personnel, Records and Welfare Section

On January 10, 1945, a letter to the Insurance and Claims Department of the United States Lines from R.H. Farinholt, Lt. Cmdr., U.S.C.G.R. (T) for the Merchant Marines says that only three men were lost in the Japanese transport, among them Walter. On October 30, 1945, the Maritime War Emergency Board issued certificates of presumptive death in the case of these three men.

The final letter is from the War Shipping Administration, dated June 3, 1946. It presents Goongsie with the Mariner's Medal and a letter in commemoration of the greatest service anyone can render cause or country.

Mom told me that sometime after Walter's death, a couple of his former shipmates came to the house and told the family about Walter's death. They said that when the *American Leader* was first sunk in September of 1942, Walter's leg was seriously hurt. They thought his knee was injured or his leg broken. Several months on a German raider boat, followed by years in the prison camp did nothing to help it, and it did not heal properly. He always had a limp thereafter. On Java, the crew was divided into two parties. One party was sent to the jungles to build a railroad. The other party included the injured, sick, or otherwise disabled. Walter was in the second group.

After years in the Java prison camp, more than 7,000 prisoners were loaded onto an old, coal-burning Japanese Transport ship, the *Junyo Maru* and sent to Malay. Walter and his mates were among them. A British submarine, the *HMS Tradewind*, torpedoed the ship. As the prisoners were swimming towards shore, Walter was trying to help someone else. The sailors said that Walter was always helping someone. He was just that type of person. They waited for him, but Walter said, "I'm fine, you go on ahead." When they looked back, he was gone.

Mom said that in the years to follow, she received a couple of postcards from people in New York City and one from Indonesia asking after Walter. What had happened to him? They missed him. Mom said the New York person was a Chinese girl. It was hard for everyone to believe that this strong, vigorous, outgoing man had perished at sea.

CODA

It is entirely fitting that in the year that this was written (2000), a memorial service was held at the site of the sinking of the *Junyo Maru.*

In early June 2000, a small Dutch navy squadron participating in joint maneuvers in Indonesian waters was scheduled to visit Jakarta. Two Dutch police officers who had lost relatives in the *Junyo Maru* disaster suggested a service. A memorial service for those sailors who perished was conducted at the actual latitude and longitude of the sinking. They wrote to Captain George Duffy beforehand and asked if he wanted to "commit something to the waters." Captain Duffy was the nineteen-year-old junior 3rd officer aboard the *American Leader* with Walter, who was the 2nd officer. He was interned in the Java camp with Walter and was aboard the *Junyo Maru* when it went down.

Captain Duffy dispatched the names of the eight Americans who had perished in that disaster. The names were to be attached to a flower cast into the Indian Ocean during the service on Sunday, June 4, 2000.

Figs. 8, 9 — Left, the ships in the squadron with white-uniformed crewmen staffing the rails and right, Ed Melis with a Dutch naval officer preparing to drop the enormous ribbon-festooned floral wreath into the sea.

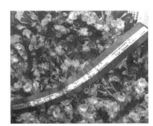

Figs. 10 — A closeup of the ribbon inscribed with the names of the eight Americans: Willie H. Dryer, Moody H. Harrison, Walter H. Lee, Philip P. McKeever, G.R. Miller, Owen H. Reed, J.R. Sokolowski and Frank E. Stallman.

Now, in the years following Walter's life, I can say that he set an example, he made me proud, and I wish that he could have been known by more people, especially Chinese. I continue to seek out his few surviving shipmates. They are scattered about the country, and most are in their eighties now. Of those who knew Walter as someone other than a sailor, only my mother remains.

CHRISTOPHER LEE

The author, center, with his mother, sister and brother.

CHILD OF TWO WORLDS

by Andrew Lam

Two roads lead to my home: one long,
yet short, the other short, yet long.
— From a Vietnamese folk song

When I was six years old, living in Vietnam, I saw Mrs. Lau, wife of our family servant, drag herself out of bed only a few hours after giving birth to bury her newborn's umbilical cord in our garden. Her gestures among the jasmine bushes, the mumbling of prayers, the burning of joss sticks, and the offerings of mangoes and rice stirred a deep sense of mystery in me. Later I asked my mother about the incident, and in a solemn voice, she announced that it was the Vietnamese way to ask the land to bless and protect the newborn. "Your umbilical cord is also buried in an earthen jar in our garden," she said. The incident and the knowledge of my own earthly ties made a strong impression on me: Our ways were sacred and very old.

In that world of parochial sanctities, I was not entirely convinced that the outside world existed. Vietnam, the tropical garden, was all there was. Life was deemed cyclical, but the world was not yet round. It hovered instead in my mind's eye in the shape of a voluptuous and ruffled *S*, the map of our country that I had more or less mastered in geography class in grammar school.

I remember standing in line each morning before class with the others—white shirts and blue shorts, all—singing at the top of our lungs the national anthem. "Oh Citizens, let's rise to this day of liberation," we would bellow. "Let's walk together, and sacrifice our lives. To avenge for our nation, we must offer our blood." I had believed in the lyric, its every word, felt that shared patriotic fervor among my young, bright-eyed peers. The war was at full throttle then, and we embraced it. In school, we devised war games in which the winners would inevitably be southerners, and the northerners were often berated for trying to invade.

No Vietnamese history book, no patriotic song, no agrarian-based adage could have possibly prophesied my own abrupt departure from Vietnam nor my subsequent transnational ending. For at the end of the Vietnam War, many of us did not die protecting river and land, as we, in our rituals, games, poetry and songs, had promised ourselves and our ancestors' spirits. For all the umbilical cords buried, for all the promises made, we did the unimaginable: We fled.

For the first time in Vietnam's embattled history, a history alleged to be 4,000 years old, the end of a war had resulted in a mass exodus. A Diaspora: refugees, boat people, the dispossessed, 2 million Vietnamese or so, scattered onto more than fifty countries across the globe.

—ɯ—

On April 28, 1975, two days before Saigon fell to the communist army and the Vietnam War ended, my family and I boarded a C-130 cargo plane full of panicked refugees and headed for Guam. I remember watching Vietnam recede into the cloudy horizon from the plane's window, a green mass of land giving way to a hazy green sea. I was almost twelve years old.

I was confused, frightened, and from all available evidence—the khaki army tents in the Guam refugee camp, the scorching heat, the long lines for army food rations, the fetid odor of the communal latrines, the freshly bulldozed ground under my sandaled feet—I was also homeless.

Places and times, when they can no longer be retrieved, tend to turn sacrosanct. Home forever lost is forever bathed in a certain twilight glow. Even after many years in America my mother still longed for the ancestral altar on which grandpa's faded black and white photo stared out into our abandoned home; she missed the carved rosewood cabinet in which she kept the enamel-covered family albums and my father's special French wines from Bordeaux; and she yearned for the antique porcelain dining set covered by faded blue silk. She fretted over the small farm we owned near the

Binh Loi bridge on the outskirts of Saigon, where the chickens roamed freely and the mangosteen and guava trees were heavy with fruits when we last visited and where the river, dotted with water hyacinths, ran swift and strong.

"This is the time of year when the guavas back home are ripened," Mother would tell the family at dinnertime.

So far from home, Mother nevertheless took her reference points in autumn, her favorite season. Autumn, the dark season, came in the form of letters she received from relatives and friends left behind. Brown and flimsy thin, like dead leaves, recycled who knows how many times, the letters threatened to dissolve with a single tear. The letters unanimously told of tragic lives: Aunty and her family barely survived; Cousin is caught for the umpteenth time trying to escape; Uncle has died from heart failure while being interrogated by the Viet Cong; yet another Uncle is indefinitely incarcerated in a malaria-infested reeducation camp; and no news yet of Cousin and family who disappeared in the South China Sea. The letters went on to inquire as to our health, then timidly asked for money, for antibiotics, for a bicycle and, if possible, for sponsorship to America. The letters confirmed what my mother, who had lived through two wars, had always known: Life is a sea of suffering, and sorrow gives meaning to life. Then, as if to anchor me in Old World tragedy, as if to bind me to that shared narrative of loss and misery, mother insisted that I, too, read those letters.

What did I do? I skimmed. I skipped. I shrugged. I put on a poker face and raked autumn in a pile and pushed it all back to her. "That country," I slowly announced in English, as if to wound, "is cursed."

That country, mind you, no longer mine. Vietnam was now so far away—an abstraction; America was now so near—outside the window, blaring on TV, written in the science fiction books that I devoured like a mad teenager—a seduction. Besides, what could a scrawny refugee teenager living in America do to save Uncle from that malaria-infested re-education camp? What could he do for Cousin and her family lost somewhere in the vast South China Sea? He could, on the other hand, pretend amnesia to save himself from grief.

My mother made the clucking sounds of disapproval with her tongue as she shook her head. She looked into my eyes and called me the worst thing she could muster, "You've become a little American now, haven't you? A cowboy." Vietnamese appropriated the word "cowboy" from the movies to imply selfishness. A cowboy in Vietnamese estimation is a rebel who, as in the spaghetti westerns, leaves town, the communal life, to ride alone into the sunset.

Mother's comment smarted, but she wasn't far from the truth. Her grievances against America had little to do with the historical, the lens through which my father, a French-educated, high-ranking officer in the South Vietnamese army, measured the world. Hers were entirely personal and, therefore, more immediate and visceral.

America had stolen her children, especially her youngest and once most-filial son. America seduced him with its optimism, twisted his thinking, bent his tongue and dulled his tropic memories. America gave him freeways and fast food and silly cartoons and sitcoms, imbuing him with sappy, happy ending incitements.

Yet it could not be helped. For the refugee child in America, the world splits perversely into two irreconcilable parts—Inside and Outside.

Inside, at home, in the crowded apartment shared by two refugee families, nostalgia ruled. Inside, the world remained dedicated to What Was.

Remember the house we used to live in, with the red bougainvillea wavering over the iron gate? Remember when we went to Hue and sailed down the Perfume for the night market and that night the sky was full of stars? Remember Tet, when Uncle showed us that trick with the cards?

Inside, the smell of fish sauce wafted along with the smell of incense from the newly built altar that housed photos of the dead—a complex smell of loss. Inside, the refugee father told and retold wartime stories to his increasingly disaffected children, reliving the battles he had fought and won, and he stirred his whiskey and soda on ice then stared blankly at the TV. Inside, the refugee mother grieved for lost relatives, lost home and hearth, lost ways of life, a whole cherished world of intimate connections, scattered and uprooted, gone, gone, all gone. And so inside often I, their refugee child, felt the collected weight of history on my shoulders, resented the legacy of a lost war, and fell silent.

Whereas Outside. . .

"What do you want to be when you grow up?" Mr. K., the English teacher in eighth grade, asked.

I never thought of the question before. Such an American question. But it intrigued. I did not hesitate. "A movie star," I answered, laughing.

Outside, I was ready to believe, to swear that the Vietnamese child who grew up in that terrible war and who saw many strange, tragic and marvelous things was someone else, not me, that it had happened in another age, centuries ago.

That Vietnamese boy never grew up, he wanders still in the tropical garden of my childhood memory, whereas I—I had gone on. Hadn't I? It was a feeling that I could not help. I came to America at a peculiar age—pubescent, and not fully formed. Old enough to remember Vietnam, I was also young enough to embrace America, and to be shaped by it.

Outside, in school, among new friends, I spoke English freely and deliberately. I whispered sweet compliments to Chinese and Filipino girls and made them blush. I cussed and joked with friends and made them laugh. I bantered and cavorted with teachers and made myself their pet.

Speaking English, I had a markedly different personality than speaking Vietnamese—a sunny, upbeat, silly and sometimes wickedly sharp-tongued kid. No sorrow, no sadness, no cataclysmic grief clung to my new language. A wild river full of possibilities flowed effortlessly from my tongue, connecting me to the New World. And I, enamored by the discovery of a newly invented self (I even gave myself a new name—"Andy, call me Andy," I would tell each new teacher and each new friend who had trouble pronouncing my Vietnamese name)—I sailed its iridescent waters toward spring.

—⟋⟍⟍—

In her suburban home with a pool shimmering in the backyard, my mother talks to ghosts. Every morning she climbs a chair and piously lights a few joss sticks for the new ancestral altar on top of the living room's bookcase and mumbles her solemn prayers to the spirits of our dead ancestors and to Buddha. On the shelves below stand my father's M.B.A. diploma, my older siblings' engineering and business degrees, my own degree in biochemistry, our combined sports trophies, and, last but not least, the latest installments of my own unending quest for self-reinvention—plaques and obelisk-shaped crystals and framed certificates—my journalism awards.

What Mother's altar and the shelves carrying their various knickknacks underneath seek to tell is the typical Vietnamese American tragicomedy, one where Old World Fatalism finally meets New World Optimism, the American Dream.

Almost half of Vietnamese living abroad ended up in North America, and the largest portion of this population resettled in California. Vietnamese immigrants, within one and a half generations, have moved from living at the receiving end of industrial revolution to being players in the information age. The second largest Vietnamese population outside of Vietnam is centered around Silicon Valley.

Ours is an epic filled with irony: The most fatalistic and sentimental people in the world found themselves relocated to a state created by fabulous fantasies, high-tech wizardry and individual ambitions.

My mother watches the smoke undulate before her eyes and sighs. She prays but she also wonders: Do ghosts cross the ocean? Do they, at least, hear her prayers amidst this world of computers, satellite dishes and modems? She does not know. But she does not like contradiction. One cannot be both this and that. She sees herself simply as a Vietnamese living in exile. She resists America as much as she can though she knows too well: She of sad ending fairy tales, in her golden years, reluctantly concedes that she may have lost this battle with America. Spring will come.

I mean, look at her now—a rejuvenated woman. Now in retirement she even goes to the gym with my father. She walks the treadmill religiously—how her fingers, fingers that once knew the blades of ripened rice and the gangrened wounds of dying soldiers, dart on the flat electronic panel of the treadmill at her spa with such ease. Mother even lifts weights.

All in all, she feels a little embarrassed that she still looks so young for a grandmother in her mid-sixties—her hair is jet black, her legs are sturdy, her arms strong and there still echoes that twang of gaiety of the teenager in her laughter. Her own mother, at her age, could barely walk. "If we were living in Vietnam now, I suppose I would sit on the wooden divan, fan myself and chew betel nuts like your grandma."

To deny her own American conversion, mother keeps a small garden. Lemongrass and mint vie for space among bitter melons, Vietnamese coriander (*rau ram*) and basil. The air in the backyard is filled with scents of home. She insists on observing death dates of her father, complete with burning paper offerings and cooking a favorite dish for the dead. Each Tet, she stays awake all night to make Vietnamese rice cakes. And she tells Vietnamese stories, drenched in sadness, to anyone willing to hear.

Consider this then as a late Norman Rockwell tableau: A sun-drenched living room in a Silicon Valley home where a Vietnamese woman sits on her sofa, telling the story of an ill-fated princess to her two wide-eyed, American-born grandchildren.

Once, she says, there was a beautiful princess who fell in love with a fisherman who sang beautiful ballads of love each morning as he sailed past her pavilion. One day the fisherman, unaware of her existence, sailed downriver to fish another kingdom. One season followed another and she, pining for his voice, fell ill and died. And in her ashes, in place of her heart, the king found a bright red ruby. He had it carved into a drinking bowl. And whenever he poured into it, the image of the fisherman appeared, sailing his boat on the water. And his voice is heard singing sweet and sad songs.

Years later, the fisherman came sailing back. He heard of this magic bowl and begged at the palace gate for entrance. Days passed and he despaired and began to sing. And his voice reached the king in his palace and the fisherman was summoned. Into the bowl, tea was poured. Then lo and behold, the fisherman watched in amazement as his own image appeared in the princess' heart. He began to weep. Had he only known of her love! Then another miracle: As one of his tears fell into the bowl, it melted into blood and disappeared.

The story, taking its cue from a tradition of fatalism, does not go down well in America—certainly not with my brother's children. Aged four and six, they resist her tragic endings. They challenge her fatalism with their American wisdom. "The princess only sleeps in the enchanted forest, Grandma. She waits for the Prince Charming kiss." My mother shakes her head and laughs. And she gives in. At her

ANDREW LAM

grandchildren's request, she slips into the VCR *The Little Mermaid* video and they watch the princess struggle toward a happily-ever-after.

What woke the Vietnamese refugee—that fleeing princess—from her millennial stupor, on the other hand, was no Prince Charming kiss but a simple yet potent idea of progression. A cliché to native-borns, the American Dream nevertheless seduces the sedentary Vietnamese to travel from halfway around the world. It's the American Dream that kissed her hard, tongued her, in fact, and in the morning she awakes to find, to her own amazement, that she can readily pronounce mortgage, escrow, aerobic, tax shelter, G.P.A., M.B.A., M.D., BMW, Porsche, overtime, stock options. Gone is the cyclical nature of her provincial thinking, and lost is her land-bound mentality. She finds that she's upwardly mobile, that she is connected to other countries by virtue of her relatives spreading across the globe and by new communication technologies. She can e-mail relatives as far away as France and Hong Kong. She can see the future.

She sees, for instance, her own restaurant in the "for rent" sign on a dilapidated store in a run-down neighborhood. She sees her kids graduating from top colleges. She imagines her own home with a pool in five years time—all things that are impossible back home. Indeed, she astonishes herself by her ambitions. We'll build a shop here, buy a house there. We'll borrow money and start a company in a few years if we work hard, really hard . . . .

And why not? Her American dream has chased away her Vietnamese nightmare. Compared to the bloody battlefields, the malaria-infested New Economic Zone, a vindictive communist regime that monitored everyone's movement, the squalid refugee camps scattered across Southeast Asia, the murders and rapes and starving and drowning on the high seas, California is paradise.

Soon enough houses are bought, jobs are had, children are born, old folks are buried and businesses are opened. A community that previously saw itself as exiled, as survivors of some historical blight, as a people born from tragedy and who are prepared to return to their homeland, to tend their abandoned ancestral graves, to face their oppressors, slowly changes its mind. Its roots are sinking deeper and deeper into the American loam.

Soon enough in San Jose, Orange County, San Diego, L.A., (not to mention Houston and Dallas), up and down the California coast, Little Saigons, economic and cultural centers that altered the existing landscapes, begin to sprout and blossom. And the stories of the horrible war and terrifying escape over the high seas that once emanated from these places slowly give way to gossip of new-found successes in the Golden Land.

Did you hear about the Vietnamese Rhodes scholar to England? He was on the *Tonight Show* with Johnny Carson.

Brother, did you know that there is a Vietnamese astronaut in N.A.S.A.?

Did you know that the first person to receive seven degrees from M.I.T. was a Vietnamese boat person, and he did it in five years!

Remember him, sister, he's now a C.E.O. for a multimillion-dollar electronic firm in Silicon Valley.

The drama of the initial expulsion is replaced by the jubilation of a new-found status and wealth. If truth be told, the letters sent from Vietnam had far less a grip on my mother than the letters she, in turn, sent back home to those left behind. Full of reports of whose son and daughter graduated *summa cum laude* and valedictorian and whose husband has become a surgeon and whose wife has become a successful real estate agent and so on, and enclosed with photos of two-story homes, of expensive and shiny sport cars in front of which tall and beautiful children stand waving and smiling to the yokel cousins they barely remember, the letters confirmed for the long-suffering relatives back home what they have suspected all along: Anything is possible in America.

A race of modern Ulysses thus responded to my mother's siren letters. In the dead of night, Vietnamese bent on an American conversion, by the hundreds, by the thousands, climb on board old rickety fishing boats for the perilous journey to America.

Here then perhaps is the final irony of that bitter war: Since the Vietnamese Diaspora began twenty-seven years ago, Vietnam, having defeated imperialistic America, fell susceptible to America's charms and seduction. In their post-war poverty and suffering, Vietnamese yearned for a new beginning in America. They want Levis, freedom, microwave, democracy, double-tiered freeways, happiness.

ANDREW LAM

They diligently remove Uncle Ho's photo from their walls, and to replace the void put up posters of *Bay Watch* and AC/DC and Kiss. They slip a video from Hong Kong or Hollywood into the VCR and marvel at the beauty and glamorous possibilities that exist in the outside world.

What has happened is that a new and radical idea had injected itself in the Vietnamese land-bound imagination. It is a powerful migratory myth, one that exhorts fabulous cosmopolitan endings. And the Vietnamese language of nationalism, too—what had for millennia given the Vietnamese unfathomable strength to endure incredible suffering to fend off foreign invaders and colonizers alike—has been subverted by a single vocabulary word: *Viet Kieu.*

Viet Kieu: Vietnamese nationals living abroad, especially those in America, whose successes and wealth serve as a mirror against which the entire nation, mired still in poverty and political oppression, reflects on its own lost potential. Uncle Ho Chi Minh once preached freedom and independence to his compatriots (though he meant independence and freedom from colonization and imperialism, not for the individual) to spur them to battle against the French and American and South Vietnamese. Today it is the *Viet Kieu*, those persecuted by Uncle Ho's followers and forced to flee, people like me, who exude that much-coveted independence and freedom.

"Go to America"—so goes the new Vietnamese mantra, where multiple reincarnations may be had in one lifetime. Go to America, and your sufferings end. Go to America, and your sons and daughters will grow up to be astronauts or presidents of rich computer companies

It happened before. Surely it will happen again.

Trung, the rice farmer's son, for instance, the one who brought only seven oranges with him onto a crowded boat thinking they should last him the whole journey across the Pacific—how big is the ocean anyway?—had escaped to America. And instead of helping the old man plant next season's crop he turned into an architect who helps design—on his brand-new laptop—glassy high-rises for cities across the globe. And Thao, the jack fruit vendor's daughter who once expected to follow her mother's footsteps, also escaped, and found herself a decade or so later in a different kind of market: Wall Street. Now Cynthia, the sophisticate, through her computer link ups, is busy negotiating across time zones, oceans, continents.

On the wall above my writing desk, there's a photograph of me taken a few years ago during one of my many trips back to Vietnam as a journalist. In it I stand at the entrance of my old house, its green iron gates are rusted beyond recognition, and the bougainvillea of my memory is gone.

Though I smile in the photo, it's a sad and knowing smile. For behind that smile is complex self-knowledge based on opposite ideas that took me a long, long time to grasp: The past is irretrievable, yet I can never be free from it. Though I can never sever myself from my childhood visions and my own sentimental longings, I have irrevocably changed.

Somewhere in between the boy who once sang the Vietnamese national anthem in the schoolyard in Saigon with tears in his eyes and the man who writes these words was the slow but natural demise of the old nationalistic impulse. The boy was willing to die for his homeland. The man had become circumspect. The boy had believed that the borders, like the Great Wall of China, were real demarcations, their integrity not to be disputed. The man discovered that the borders have always been porous. The boy was once overwhelmed by the tragedy that had fallen on his people, had resented history for robbing him and his family of home and hearth and national identity. The man, though envious of the primacy of his childhood emotions, has become emboldened by his own process of individualization.

And yet this much is true also: were it not for my ties to the Vietnamese people, their trial and tribulation, were it not for my own memories of the life that was taken from me, my American individuality would be shallow.

Often, I wonder why my Vietnamese childhood seems full of magic and why—though I am no longer beholden to the reality of my homeland with her many current troubles and problems—my memory of her continues to inform and inspire me. There are no easy answers to this, of course, but I think it has to do with that deep sense of reverence I once felt toward the land in which my umbilical cord is buried.

ANDREW LAM

After all, to live in a less than modern society where land still holds your imagination, where ties are permanent and where tradition is concrete, is, in a way, to live in an enchanted world. It's normal that your ancestors' ghosts talk to you in your dreams, that they inhabit all sort of corners of your house, and that you should answer them in your prayers, in your offerings, in the incense smoke you burn nightly. In that world, omens are to be read from the wind, and the butterfly that comes hovering above the altar or lands on your shoulder is the spirit of your grandfather. On a certain day of the year, you do not leave the house for fear of bad luck, then on another the entire family flocks to the cemetery to burn offerings and cut the grass of grandpa's grave to appease him in the spirit world.

Which is to say, Vietnam was once for me a world full of deep mystery, and I lived then in awe with the hallowed land, its powers.

And then no more.

The greatest phenomenon in this century, I am now convinced, has little to do with the world wars but with the dispossessed they sent fleeing: The Cold War and its aftermath has given birth to a race of children born "elsewhere," of transnationals whose memories are layered and whose biographies transgress the borders.

Globalization for me means, among other things, a world awash with people whose displaced lives mock the idea of borders—they are prophets of migration, moving from language to language, sensibility to sensibility, constantly in flux, shifting. And if the Vietnamese refugee left Vietnam under the shadow of history, he also, in the blink of an eye, became the first global villager by default. The trauma of his leaving, the effort he makes in claiming and creating a new place for himself in a quickly shifting world, his ability to negotiate himself in an age of open systems and melting borders makes him the primary character in the contemporary global novel.

My sense of home these days seems to have less to do with geography than imagination and memories. Home is portable if one is in commune with one's soul. I no longer see my identity as a fixed thing but something in constant flux. What lies before me then is a vision of continents overlapping and of crisscrossing traditions. Call it a new American frontier if you will, but one chased by a particular transpacific sensibility. For mine is a landscape where Saigon, New York and Paris intersect, where the Perfume River of Hue flows under the Golden Gate Bridge.

I applaud Edward Said, the cultural critic who suggests that if one wishes to transcend his provincial and national limits, one should not reject attachments to the past but work through them. Irretrievable, the past must be mourned and remembered and assimilated. To truly grieve the loss of a nation and the robbed history of a banished people, that old umbilical cord must be unearthed and, through the task of art, through the act of imagination, woven into a new living tapestry.

Trung, the farmer turned architect, knows something of this. Perhaps that is why he paints late at night. On his large canvasses, blurred figurines, amid a sea of colors, dance, mourn, contemplate, or simply gawk at the stars. What Trung knows but cannot say is that some psychic disconnection occurred the moment he left the rice field to embrace a new cosmopolitan reality. Yet something survived. Call it restlessness of the soul. And though he designs homes and high-rises by day, at night he paints like a demon.

Another friend, a poet who left Vietnam at age seven, tells me his unfinished book of poetry is his true home. It is the only thing he takes with him as he travels. I've read his poems. They are dark and lyrical, yet void of rancor. They range instead like clouds or rain as to create a new space—his words are to replace lost land— for all displaced souls to dwell.

And me—each morning I write. I long for freedom. I yearn for memory. And only this morning as I type these words does it occur to me that mine too, strangely enough, is a kind of filial impulse, an effort to reconcile between spring and autumn, between my agricultural past and my cosmopolitan future.

Still, I shudder at the irony. The sounds of my fingers gliding on the keyboard remind me of the solemnity of my mother's morning prayers. When I was younger, I found mother's story of the weeping fisherman and his dead princess morbid— so much death and blood and sorrow seem to plague the Vietnamese narratives, even those told to children. Only now, approaching middle age, do I recognize that the sad tale is, in its own wise way, one of requited love.

"Tell me, where are you from?" the platinum blond in a black Donna Karan dress asked me at a recent cocktail party in a Russian Hill villa. I gestured my martini to the shimmering bay outside the French window and smiled. "Over there, long ago."

"Oh!" she said. She did not know what to make of such an opaque answer or how to reconcile the sadness in my voice with the gesture and the smile. What I was not willing to divulge at such a festive event is that somewhere in between "here" and "over there" a part of me ceased to exist.

In my mind now, I see him as if in a newsreel. See him standing on the beach in Guam at sunset, a small boy staring westward, the waves lapping at his feet, tears in his eyes. A day after Saigon fell, and he is all alone. See him raise his hand, reluctantly, shyly, and wave good-bye to that S-shaped land. He waves some more, as if somehow this overzealous gesture will alleviate his sorrow. But then his eyes begin to wander. He notices the glowing soda pop machines by the army PX with all the choices— Coca-Cola, Pepsi, Dr Pepper. He is mesmerized by their colorful glows, so beautiful and entrancing. He is awed. Then he hears two young GIs joking with one another as they stroll toward their sports car. He grows curious about the language of the young men. It's full of laughter and bantering, a seductive song to his ears. He feels his tongue curling inside his mouth, forming new words, new names of things. His eyes follow them as they drive out the refugee camp down the smooth freeway. The sun is almost gone now, a tiny golden arc over a darkening sea. On the red sand, the boy's shadow elongates. He turns then, toward the open road. Takes a step. Then another. And the sun disappears entirely. And he, too, is gone.

TOPOGRAPHY OF WAR DONORS

Margaret Abraham

Andrew H. Brimmer

Min Chan

Arthur Chang & Allison Thrush

Terrence Cheng

Curtis Chin & Jeff Kim

Jeff Chou

David L. Eng

Luis Francia & Midori Yamamura

Jessica Hagedorn

Kin & Betty Hamashige

Amy Hill

Gayle Isa

Amy Jedlicka

Peter Kiang

Eugenia Kim

Holly Kim & Phil Price

Paul Lai

Pairote Laochumroonvorapong &
　　Richard Lucas

Fay Ann Lee

Marie G. Lee

Min Jin Lee

Jeffrey D. Leong

Sunaina Maira

Betty Ng

Kien Nguyen

N. Rain Noe

Brandon Rush

Anantha Sudhakar

Herb Tsuchiya

Jonathan Van Meter

Grace Lyu Volckhausen

Dora Wang

Michael Yi

Sarah Midori Zimmerman

Publication of this volume is supported by a major grant from the CJ Huang Foundation.
Additional support provided by The New York State Council on the Arts,
The Rockefeller Brothers Fund and The Jerome Foundation.

ACKNOWLEDGEMENTS

We are enormously grateful for all the hard work and good faith that so many people, especially the writers, offered to make this book happen. The road to publication is a long one, and we are happy to have had so many friends along the way.

We wish to thank the staff members of The Asian American Writers' Workshop who lent their support in ways large and small: Executive Director Quang Bao, Administrative Director Jeannie Wong and Publications Director Noel Shaw, as well as Anantha Sudhakar, Kavita Rajanna, Adrian Leung and Pimpila Thanaporn. Countless interns have helped behind the scenes, including Debra Augustine, Dawn Chan, Miren Anna Garamendi, Anjali Goyal, Jennifer Ku, Elizabeth Lee, Melissa Leviste, Rajal Pitroda, Di Shui, Chinua Akimaro Thelwell, Patricia Justine Tumang, Kathy Yoo and Shelly Wong.

And a special shout of thanks to Patrick Keppel, for copyediting all the way from Brattleboro, Vermont, and to Jeffrey Lin for his elegant design.

Also, we'd like to take a moment to acknowledge the life and work of Iris Chang (1968-2004), who told the war stories of so many.

CONTRIBUTORS

Elsa Arnett was born in Saigon to a Vietnamese mother and a New Zealand father. Her poetry and personal essays have appeared in *The Asian Pacific American Journal*, the *Crab Orchard Review*, *Connections*, *Terminus*, *Pearl*, *River Teeth*, the *Sierra Nevada College Review*, and the Italian journal *Internazionale*. She lives in the San Francisco Bay Area.

Shymala Dason grew up in Malaysia, is an alumna of Bennington College, and came to writing via a detour that includes an M.A. in Applied Mathematics and a decade of working on various atmospheric science projects at N.A.S.A. She has published short fiction and non-fiction, contributing to the *Massachusetts Review* and Marion Zimmer Bradley's *Fantasy Magazine*. She is currently working on a novel about a Malaysian expat family, like hers, who is scattered around the world. She is writing about the tension of their immigrant experiences, from transplant shock and the challenges of crossing racial and class barriers to the chasms of mutual bewilderment that open up between close kin who live and grow far apart. She can be found on the Internet at shymala.com.

Xujun Eberlein grew up in China, moved to the United States in 1988, and received her Ph.D. from the Massachusetts Institute of Technology in 1995. Her stories can be found in *Story Quarterly*, *Stand* (U.K.), *Meridians*, *The Saint Ann's Review*, *Night Train*, and *Cottonwood*, among others. Two of her stories received awards from the Writer's Digest Annual Writing Competition and the William Faulkner Creative Writing Competition. She is currently completing her story collection, *Swimming with Mao*.

Jennifer F. Estaris is currently working on a novel based on her essay in this anthology. Her work has appeared in *Really Small Talk*, *Lit Rag*, *Good Use*, *Mosaic*, and *Sassy*, among others. She is a candidate for an M.F.A. in creative writing at Columbia University.

A poet, nonfiction writer, and teacher who lives in New York City, **Luis H. Francia** is the author, most recently, of the poetry collection *Museum of Absences* (Manila and San Francisco: University of the Philippines Press and Meritage Press, 2004). His semiautobiographical critique of the Philippines, where he grew up, *Eye of the Fish: A Personal Archipelago* (Kaya Press, 2001), won both the 2002 PEN Center Open Book Award and the 2002 Asian American Literary Award. Other books include *The Arctic Archipelago and Other Poems* (Manila: Ateneo de Manila University Press, 1992) and *Memories of Overdevelopment: Reviews and Essays of Two Decades* (Anvil Press, 1998). He is the editor of *Brown River, White Ocean: A Twentieth Century Anthology of Philippine Literature in English* (Rutgers University Press, 1993); with Eric Gamalinda as coeditor, *Flippin': Filipinos on America* (Asian American Writers' Workshop, 1996); and, with Angel Velasco Shaw as coeditor, *Vestiges of War: The Philippine-American War and the Aftermath of an Imperial Dream 1899-1999* (New York University Press, 2002). He has taught Asian American literature at Sarah Lawrence College, the University of Hawaii in Honolulu, and currently teaches at the Asian/Pacific/American Studies Institute at New York University. He writes for *The Nation*, the *Village Voice*, and the *Inquirer Sunday Magazine* in Manila.

Andrew Lam is a syndicated writer and an editor with the Pacific News Service, a short story writer, and a regular commentator on National Public Radio's *All Things Considered*. He co-founded New California Media, an association of four hundred ethnic media in California. His essays have appeared in dozens of newspapers across the country, including the *New York Times*, the *L.A. Times*, the *San Francisco Chronicle*, the *Baltimore Sun*, the *Atlanta Journal*, and the *Chicago Tribune*. He has also written essays for such magazines as *Mother Jones*, *The Nation*, *San Francisco Focus*, *Proult Journal*, *In Context*, and *Earth Island Journal*. His short stories have been published in *Manoa Journal*, *Crab Orchard Review*, *Nimrod International*, *Michigan Quarterly West*, *Zyzzyva*, *Transfer Magazine*, and many others. Lam was a John S. Knight Fellow at Stanford University during the academic year 2001-02, studying journalism, and was featured in the PBS documentary, *My Journey Home*, in which a film crew followed him back to Vietnam. His book *Perfume Dreams: Writings on the Vietnamese Diaspora* was published by Heyday Books in 2005.

Christopher Lee, a first generation Chinese American, born in San Francisco, California, has lived in Oregon for the past twenty-eight years. He is a music director, having been a librarian, a technical writer, a carpenter, an organ builder, and a singing telegram messenger. His articles have appeared in the *Journal of the American Library Association*, *Valley Parent Magazine*, and the Chinese Historical Society of Southern California.

Johnny Lew (editor) is a doctoral candidate in American and New England Studies at Boston University. Now based in New York, Lew's research is on the history and politics of American travel and migration literature. He has taught at Boston University, Babson College, LaGuardia Community College, and Rutgers-Newark University. Lew received his bachelor's degree in English literature from Vassar College in 1993.

Maya Lin is internationally recognized in both the fields of art and architecture. Since establishing her studio practice in New York in 1986, she has created monuments, sculptures, architecture and design objects that have been "proposing ways of thinking and imagining that resist categories, genres, and borders" (Michael Brenson). The numerous rewards she has received include the American Institute of Architects Honor Award, 1982; the American Institute of Architecture's Henry Bacon Memorial Award, 1982; the American Academy of Arts and Letters Award in Architecture, 1996; and most recently, the first Finn Juhl Prize in architecture in Denmark, 2003. Lin's life and work were detailed in the Academy Award-winning documentary film, *Maya Lin: A Strong Clear Vision* (1995). Her artwork has been shown in numerous solo exhibitions including the Wexner Center for the Arts, the Grey Art Gallery, the Kunstindustrimuseet in Copenhagen, the American Academy in Rome, and the Cooper Union. She is represented by Gagosian Gallery.

Andrea Louie (editor) is the author of a novel, *Moon Cakes* (Ballantine Books, 1995). In 2003 she was a recipient of a Ludwig Volgelstein Foundation grant in fiction, was short-listed for the Rona Jaffe Foundation Writers' Award and served as a writer-in-residence for the National Book Foundation. She has also been a recipient of a New York Foundation for the Arts fellowship in nonfiction and was named honorable mention in Francis Ford Coppola's Zoetrope All-Story Short Fiction Contest. She has been awarded artist residencies at Yaddo, the MacDowell Colony, Djerassi, Hedgebrook and the Fundacíon Valparáiso in Spain. She is currently a staff writer at Brooklyn College and has taught creative nonfiction in the youth programs at The Asian American Writers' Workshop and at the Hamilton-Madison Settlement House in New York City's Chinatown.

The son of Vietnamese refugees, **Dang Ngo** is a professional photographer who has been campaigning on behalf of the Burmese people for more than twelve years. In the last five years he's devoted the majority of his time to both documenting the human rights struggle in Burma and delivering medicine and supplies to refugees and internally displaced peoples along the Thai-Burma border. Dang's work has been published in many international magazines, and he's served as a documentary photographer for such organizations as Greenpeace and Backpack Medics. He is represented by ZUMA Press.

Gary Reyes has been a newspaper photojournalist for more than twenty years. He began his career working for small daily newspapers in Northern California. He was hired as a staff photographer for the *Oakland* (CA) *Tribune* in 1985. His seven-year stint there included the 1990 Pulitzer Prize for Spot News Photography by the *Oakland Tribune* photography staff for their coverage of the devastating Loma Prieta Earthquake. He also worked as a staff photographer for the *Sacramento Bee*, his hometown newspaper, before joining the photography staff of the *San Jose Mercury News* in 1993. Reyes is a graduate of California State University, Sacramento.

Rahna Reiko Rizzuto is the author of the novel *Why She Left Us* (HarperCollins, 1999; winner of the American Book Award) and the recipient of the U.S. Japan Creative Artist Fellowship, funded by the National Endowment for the Arts. She was associate editor of *The NuyorAsian Anthology: Asian American Writings About New York City* (The Asian American Writers' Workshop, 1999). Her work has appeared in numerous publications, including the *L.A. Times*, and is forthcoming in the anthology, *Because I Said So: 33 Mothers Write about Children, Sex, Men, Aging, Race and Themselves* (HarperCollins, 2005). She teaches in the M.F.A. program for creative writing at Goddard College and is currently working on her second book *If Hiroshima in the Morning*.

Originally from Detroit, **Michael Sandoval** has called New York City his home for many years. He completed New York University's M.F.A. program in film and currently works as a teacher and freelancer in the independent film world. In addition, he directs a media program for preparatory school youth in the city. Michael's films have won such awards as a competition screening at the Berlin Film Festival, an audience award at Palm Springs, and Best Screenplay at the Arrivano Y Corto Film Festival in Italy. Sandoval graduated from Brown University and received an M.F.A. in fiction writing from the University of Michigan.

Anooradha Iyer Siddiqi was born in Madras, India, and fell in love with architecture very soon afterward. She studied literature at Georgetown University and architecture at the University of Washington. She worked most recently at Rafael Viñoly Architects on the Center for Science and Computation at Bard College, Jazz at Lincoln Center, and the Institute for Genomics at Princeton University. Her private practice spans architecture and design projects in the United States and India, including the Manhattan loft renovation for The Asian American Writers' Workshop. She is currently assistant professor in the Department of Architecture at the Wentworth Institute of Technology and instructor at the Boston Architectural Center. Her loving parents, her spectacular brother, and her husband's wonderful family are her role models. She lives in New York City and Cambridge with her husband Asif.

Born in Saigon, Vietnam in 1972, **John Vu** arrived to the United States in 1980 after one and a half years in refugee camps in Malaysia and the Philippines. He is currently working as a research analyst. He has done consulting work for companies, nonprofit foundations and the U.S. Department of Justice. He holds a Masters in Program Design and Evaluation from Claremont Graduate University and an M.B.A. from the Peter Drucker School of Management. John lives in San Francisco and is currently working on a photo book about Vietnam in which he explores a personal relationship with a country in the midst of profound change.

Dora Wang, M.D., was the recipient of a Lannan Foundation Residency for Creative Writing in 2002. She is an assistant professor of psychiatry at the University of New Mexico School of Medicine. She received her M.A. in English from the University of California at Berkeley and her M.D. from the Yale School of Medicine.